D1569183

HARVEST HOUSE PUBLISHERS
Eugene, Oregon 97402

WALK THRU THE BIBLE
Atlanta, Georgia 30341

Cover by Paz Design Group, Salem, Oregon

LIFEWALK
Copyright © 1998 by Walk Thru the Bible Ministries
Published by Harvest House Publishers
Eugene, OR 97402

Library of Congress Cataloging-in-Publication Data

   Lifewalk / Walk Thru the Bible Ministries.
      p. cm.
   ISBN 1-56507-911-6 (trade paper)
    1. Meditations. 2. Devotional calendars. I. Walk Thru the Bible
(Educational ministry)
BV4811.L53 1998
242'.2—dc21   98-5768
                                                      CIP

98 99 00 01 02 03 / DH / 10 9 8 7 6 5 4 3 2 1

Contents

Introduction

Like an icy sports drink on a hot summer day, *LifeWalk* refreshes and replenishes your thirsty soul. Just as quickly as having a cool drink, you are ushered into the presence of God, offered hope, encouragement, and nuggets of spiritual food to restore your faith, focus your attention, improve your serve, and lighten your load. In less time than it takes to brew a cup of coffee, your *LifeWalk* reading provides insight into spiritual truth and applies that truth to your hectic life.

These daily readings (one for the weekend) are taken from the devotional magazine *LifeWalk*, which has been faithfully produced and distributed by the publishing team at Walk Thru the Bible since 1990. The result is truly a team effort involving the creative insights and hard work of a very dedicated group. Special thanks go to Editorial Director Paula Kirk; writers Martha Comeaux, Kyle Henderson, Mark Littleton, Len Woods; designer Michelle Strickland; and all who have contributed over the years.

Walk Thru the Bible is pleased to join our friends at Harvest House in making this book available to you. It is our prayer that through *LifeWalk* God may call you into a closer walk with Him.

Life's Goals

Faithfulness

Why are dogs called "man's best friend"?
Dogs are loyal to their masters, eager to serve,
and always ready to defend. In a word,
dogs are faithful.

How does your *faithfulness* to God
compare with that? Are you loyal to Christ,
eager to serve His church, and ready to
defend His name?

During your quiet times this week,
ask God to strengthen your faithfulness
to Him and to those around you.

God Rewards Our Faithfulness

Read
REVELATION 2:19

Being faithful to Christ means obeying Him now more than you did at first.

Your World A little stray dog approached a sentinel of the Scots Guards outside James Palace. The dog was cold and hungry, and finally the sentry picked him up and fed him. Soon "Jack," as he was called, became the mascot of the Scots Guards and went everywhere with his master during the Crimean War.

When the soldier was killed in battle, his comrades found Jack loyally standing beside him. Queen Victoria was so moved by the story that she awarded Jack a miniature Victoria Cross, which was affixed to his collar.

God's Word Though only a dog, Jack possessed a virtue that seems to be in short supply today: faithfulness.

The Queen of England rewarded Jack for his faithfulness; likewise, the King of kings blesses His faithful people.

> As you know, we consider blessed those who have persevered. You have heard of Job's perseverance and have seen what the Lord finally brought about. The Lord is full of compassion and mercy (James 5:11).

Your Walk Be honest: Are you faithful like Job?

Begin your walk of faithfulness by covenanting with the Lord. Promise God that you will strive to faithfully face the problems of life. Then ask Him to help you keep your promise. You can take God at His Word; He will help you and reward you.

God's Great Faithfulness

Read
PSALM 89:1-4

*God's faithfulness
toward us
never fails,
even when we
fail Him.*

Your World One writer has written of finding two doves by a roadway. One was dead. Its mate, though, was unwilling to leave the corpse.

The man picked up the living dove and threw it into the air, expecting to watch the dove fly away. But the loyal bird came back.

He then gently put the bird in his car and drove several miles away. Upon being released from the car, the bird immediately flew back in the direction of its dead mate.

Later, on his way home, he found the second dove with the first. But this time neither was alive. The dove was faithful unto death.

God's Word In the midst of Jeremiah's mourning over the destruction of Jerusalem, he wrote, "Because of the LORD's great love we are not consumed, for his compassions never fail. They are new every morning; great is your faithfulness" (Lamentations 3:22-23).

Like the tenacious dove, God's faithfulness to us was unto death. He did not simply reject us in anger. He gave His Son to die so that we might be reconciled to Him and renewed.

Your Walk If God required such of Himself, can He ask any less of us? Fortunately, He does not require a torturous death of all of His children. But He does require faithfulness. And He does promise to give us the power to be faithful through the Holy Spirit.

11

Well Done, Faithful Servant

Read
HEBREWS 11:8-10

*Faithfulness
is reaching
a faraway
destination with
many small
steps.*

Your World By the time the Scottish Reformer John Knox reached his forties, he had seen glorious days of revival and preached some of the greatest sermons in history. But as he grew older, his ministry became less spectacular; the glory days were past.

Nevertheless, Knox wrote in his journal, "I shall hoe the ground that God has given me. And perhaps by His grace, He shall ignite me again. But ignite me or not, by His grace, I shall hoe the ground."

God's Word Undoubtedly, Knox will one day hear these words of Jesus: "Well done, good and faithful servant! You have been faithful with a few things; I will put you in charge of many things. Come and share your master's happiness!" (Matthew 25:21).

Yes, Knox will be rewarded for his mighty works. But Jesus won't forget his faithfulness in less-heralded works.

Your Walk Have you ever been on an exercise program? If you have, you know that a hard workout every week or two isn't nearly as effective as a shorter workout done every day.

Faithfulness is like a marathoner running for the finish line. For miles and miles he plods along. True, he may not be as fast as the sprinter, but he runs with endurance. And in a marathon, one who endures receives the prize.

How are you running?

To Whom Much Is Given

Read
JAMES 3:1

Only God can make a faithful leader, but a faithful leader will please God.

Your World In Old Testament times, the high priest had to perform his rituals and rites without mistakes. He had to be precise. He had to serve by the rules revealed in God's Word.

Though ministers in the church today aren't required to obey the ceremonies of the Old Testament, they are still responsible for ministering according to God's Word. Faithfulness on the part of our leaders is critical. We rely on the accuracy of their knowledge and wisdom in leading us in matters of faith and practice.

God's Word The apostle Paul considered the Christian ministry to be not only a great privilege but an awesome responsibility. He wrote, "Now it is required that those who have been given a trust must prove faithful" (1 Corinthians 4:2).

How is faithfulness demonstrated in a leader? First, by accuracy in handling the Word of God (2 Timothy 2:15). Second, by endurance in the work even through persecution (Revelation 2:10).

Your Walk Here are two ideas that will encourage your minister and help him fulfill the task God has given him. First, as a church or church-school group, give your pastor a monthly book allowance for books that will help him minister to you. Second, tell him in a note or in person that you are praying for him regularly.

13

The Search for Reliable People

Read
PROVERBS 21:5

Christ has placed the preaching of the gospel in the hands of reliable people.

Your World F. M. Young said, "It isn't the incompetent who destroy an organization. The incompetent never get into a position to destroy it. It is those who have achieved something and want to rest upon their achievements who are forever clogging things up."

God's Word One of the great needs addressed in the New Testament is the search for and nurture of reliable Christians—faithful, enduring people of God who are willing to work for His kingdom. The apostle Paul encouraged his student Timothy to seek out such people and train them: "The things you have heard me say in the presence of many witnesses entrust to reliable men who will also be qualified to teach others" (2 Timothy 2:2).

Some have noted that Paul speaks of four generations of disciples:

1. Me (Paul)
2. You (Timothy)
3. Reliable men (Timothy's disciples)
4. Others (Timothy's disciples' disciples)

Your Walk It's a remarkable process—one by which the church has been built for centuries. Discipleship isn't exclusively the job of the pastor. Discipleship is every Christian's job.

Do you want to grow? Spend regular time with a more mature Christian. Do you want to bear fruit? Spend the same kind of time with a less mature believer.

The Faithful Christ

Read
PSALM 92

Because of Christ's faithfulness, we have the power to be faithful, too.

We've looked at a number of the elements of faithfulness this week. But to really grasp what faithfulness means, we need to consider the perfect picture of faithfulness: Jesus.

He is the faithful Shepherd who seeks the straying sheep. He is the faithful Savior who paid the price of our redemption. He is the faithful Priest who comes before God's throne on our behalf. He is the faithful King who rules His subjects with justice, integrity, and love.

There's much more to learn about the faithfulness of Christ. But you know enough to know that He is worthy of your worship.

Perhaps you need to stop right now and simply thank and praise Him for His faithfulness—the faithfulness that resulted in your salvation. Because of His faithfulness, you now have life, hope, joy, love, and every other good gift He has given you. Because of His faithfulness, you have every reason to sing, dance, shout, clap, and praise His holy name.

"It is good to praise the LORD and make music to your name, O Most High, to proclaim your love in the morning and your faithfulness at night" (Psalm 92:1-2).

*What
mountain has
God chosen
for you
to scale
with Him?*

Success

Success means different things to different
people. It can mean wealth, fame, love, saving
money, winning people to Christ, climbing
Mount Everest, or having a baby. In each
case, commitment, discipline, and some
risks are required.

What is your definition of *success?*
There is no greater success than fulfilling God's
will for your life. This week, ask God to guide
you as you set short- and long-term goals.
Then during your quiet times pray that He
will bless your efforts to fulfill His will.

You Can Be Like a Tree

Read
PSALM 1

The key to success is applying God's Word in all the circumstances of life.

Your World Someone has said that the major elements of success are:

- to be able to carry money without spending it;
- to be able to act kindly, even to people who don't deserve it;
- to be able to stay on the job until it is finished;
- to be able to do one's duty even when one is not watched;
- to be able to accept criticism and improve from it.

Perhaps those qualities can be summed up as self-control, love, diligence, commitment, and wisdom.

God's Word The Bible puts it this way: A successful person is "like a tree planted by streams of water, which yields its fruit in season and whose leaf does not wither. Whatever he does prospers" (Psalm 1:3).

How does a person become a successful "tree"? "His delight is in the law of the LORD, and on his law he meditates day and night" (Psalm 1:2).

Your Walk The Word of God is God's revelation, and thus the ultimate source of direction, morality, and wisdom. By regularly meditating on it, we become the kind of people God desires—and therefore, successful.

Take some time now to meditate on Psalm 1:3. The man or woman of God is stable, secure, content, fruitful. Are you? If not, decide to spend time every day meditating on God's Word.

Success Control? Self-Control!

Read
PROVERBS 18:2

He who sows to please the Spirit will reap the Spirit's fruit of self-control.

Your World Ben King's business professor gave the class a strange assignment. For one week Ben had to record in a journal every instance in which he exercised any type of self-control. Ben also had to record how much money his self-control saved him.

When the week was over and Ben read his journal, he was astonished! He had saved over 30 dollars by keeping money in his pocket in circumstances where he normally would have spent it.

God's Word Through his experiment, Ben discovered what the Bible has taught for centuries, namely,

- that self-control is a mark of wisdom: "A fool gives full vent to his anger, but a wise man keeps himself under control" (Proverbs 29:11); and

- that wisdom is a mark of success: "I, wisdom, dwell together with prudence. . . . Blessed is the man who listens to me, . . . for whoever finds me finds life and receives favor from the LORD" (Proverbs 8:12, 34-35).

Your Walk Whether your profession is sales, engineering, medicine, education, homemaking, or any other, you can't be a success without the wisdom of self-control. Are you more like Ben before or after the assignment? Here's good news: The power of God's Spirit lives within you to give you wisdom and self-control. A richer harvest of that fruit is available to anyone who sincerely asks.

Getting Along with People

Read
Matthew 5:1-12

Make your attitude "give" instead of "get," and God will reward you.

Your World Theodore Roosevelt was a successful man. He accomplished goals that few people even dream of. At different times in his life, he was a military hero, governor of New York, president of the United States, and a Nobel peace prize winner.

When asked about his secret to success, Roosevelt had a surprising answer: "The most important ingredient in the formula of success is knowing how to get along with people."

God's Word Do people really benefit from treating others unkindly? Is an overbearing, critical, looking-out-for-number-one attitude really the way to achieve success?

Not in the long run. The writer of Proverbs reminds us that treating others with love and respect brings success, but treating them with contempt breeds failure: "A kind man benefits himself, but a cruel man brings trouble on himself" (Proverbs 11:17).

Your Walk The Proverbs are general principles, not particular promises. But as a general rule, an attitude of loving concern for others will benefit you, just as a critical, selfish attitude will do you harm.

Everyone stumbles, of course. But as a habit of life, are you kind to other people? You can be confident that if you show mercy, mercy will be shown to you.

Diligence versus Laziness

Read
NEHEMIAH 4:1-23

This contest called life is a grueling marathon, not a 100-yard dash.

Your World It's been said that success is 10 percent inspiration and 90 percent perspiration. In other words, success is due to stick-to-it-iveness more than it is due to talent.

From wealthy Wall Street magnates to university professors with doctorates, from famous entertainers to professional athletes, from Pulitzer-prize-winning journalists to Oscar-winning screenwriters, one quality is universally hailed as critical to achieving difficult goals: diligence. After all, if someone isn't willing to finish the job, why start it?

God's Word The writer of Proverbs frequently comments on the radically different effects of diligence and laziness. Here are a few examples:

- "Lazy hands make a man poor, but diligent hands bring wealth" (10:4).

- "He who works his land will have abundant food, but he who chases fantasies lacks judgment" (12:11).

- "Diligent hands will rule, but laziness ends in slave labor" (12:24).

Your Walk Are there projects in your life that you started with zeal and then put on the shelf when they got difficult? God is pleased when you stick with a task until it's finished.

Perhaps it's time to take one of those projects from the shelf, blow off the dust, and pick up where you left off. A difficult task may even bring you to tears, but when you complete it, you'll jump for joy.

Success Without Integrity?

Read
MATTHEW 16:21-28

The world measures success merely in dollars; God measures it in character.

Your World He was 36 years old and a U.S. congressman. He had everything he dreamed of as a high-school debate champion. He had everything he worked for as a summa cum laude political science undergraduate. He had everything he trained for as a brilliant Ivy League law student.

But he lost it all in a scandal with public funds. The ex-congressman couldn't maintain his success without integrity.

God's Word To some people, if a choice between maintaining Christian integrity and moving up the success ladder must be made, the choice is obvious: Forget integrity. Jesus had a different point of view about the relative value of following Him and following riches: "What good will it be for a man if he gains the whole world, yet forfeits his soul? Or what can a man give in exchange for his soul?" (Matthew 16:26).

Your Walk The ex-congressman's world came crashing down in this life. But God doesn't always do it that way. Some people who have lied and cheated won't get their just reward until Judgment Day—but they will get it.

God will richly bless a person—both in this life and in the life to come—who works diligently, works well, and works with integrity. Are you that kind of person?

God's Blessings

Read
PROVERBS 14:11

*Success
without God's
blessing is
no success
at all.*

We all want to prosper, live well, and have the "good things in life." There's nothing wrong with that. God wants to bless us with the good things He has created.

How can we receive God's blessing? Consider what God said to Joshua soon after he succeeded Moses: "Do not let this Book of the Law depart from your mouth; meditate on it day and night, so that you may be careful to do everything written in it. Then you will be prosperous and successful" (Joshua 1:8).

Notice the progression. First, Joshua was to study the Scriptures diligently—to the degree that his speech would be filled with God's law.

Second, he was to meditate on God's Word day and night. He was to think about what he read in the Bible until he understood its application in his life and the lives of God's people.

Third, he was to obey God's Word by applying it in his life. Every problem called for a look into the Book. Every situation required a thoughtful inspection of the truth and an action based on truth.

In other words, if Joshua would obey God's Word in the task to which God had called him, Joshua would be prosperous and successful. He would victoriously accomplish the task God had given him.

Joshua's story ended happily: He did obey, and God greatly blessed him.

Follow Joshua's example, and your story can end happily, too.

Excellence

What do you think of when you hear the word
excellence? An olympic ice skater executing a
perfect triple axle? Isaac Stern performing mas-
terfully on the violin? The Apollo astronauts
skipping on the moon's surface?

Excellence is not limited to the rich and
famous. In fact, none of these people would
have achieved what they did if they hadn't
decided to strive for excellence.

They worked very hard . . . and never surren-
dered their dreams to mediocrity.

As we look at excellence this week, ask God to
show you what He wants to make excellent in
your life. Then during your quiet times
pray for the necessary endurance.

Attitude: the Key to Excellence

Read
COLOSSIANS 3:15-17

An exciting life of excellence is within your grasp. Reach out and grab it.

Your World   William James said, "Compared with what we ought to be, we are only half awake. Our fires are damped, our drafts are checked. We are making use of only a small part of our possible mental and physical resources."

God's Word   A life of excellence has nothing to do with appearance, financial status, education, physical strength, or pedigree. Excellence is an attitude, a way of thinking, that pleases God.

> Finally, brothers, whatever is true, whatever is noble, whatever is right, whatever is pure, whatever is lovely, whatever is admirable—if anything is excellent or praiseworthy—think about such things (Philippians 4:8).

Your Walk   Where in your life do you desire excellence? Whether it be your job, your marriage, your health, or your relationship with God, you have already been commanded to pursue excellence—not in just one area, but in all areas.

God calls Christians to live according to a standard of excellence. And that involves hard work, sacrifice, endurance, and patience. Are you willing to pay that price? Or would you prefer to live within your self-imposed boundaries, to live life "half awake"?

As you learn more about what the Bible says about excellence, ask God to give you a heart that burns to achieve its highest potential.

The Importance of Setting Goals

Read
1 CORINTHIANS 14:12

Satisfaction comes not from just achieving a goal, but pursuing it.

Your World Few people are accidentally excellent at something. A life of excellence is marked by thoughtful planning and goal-setting—a realistic approach to achievement.

More often than not, people who excel are those who 1) set clear-cut goals, and 2) focus their energy, time, and other resources into achieving those goals.

God's Word The apostle Paul encourages believers to determine specific goals for every aspect of their lives, especially in their service to God: "Since you are eager to have spiritual gifts, try to excel in gifts that build up the church" (1 Corinthians 14:12).

Your Walk Commit an area of your life to a standard of excellence. Just dreaming about it will never make it happen. It must be important enough for you to be willing to sacrifice and work hard. Then pursue it.

Starting today, set aside 30 minutes every day to do whatever is necessary to help you achieve that goal. If it's a weight problem, go for a walk. If it's your relationship with God, pray and read the Bible. If it's your relationship with your spouse, children, or neighbor, spend that time talking to or praying for that person. And expect results.

And if you don't know what your spiritual gift is, ask God to reveal it to you this week. Then heed the words of the apostle Paul and seek to excel in it for the glory of God and His church.

God Turns Mistakes into Glory

Read
JOHN 21:15-19

Mistakes are not failures but lessons we need never learn again.

Your World Two of Thomas Edison's assistants dejectedly approached him. "We've just completed our seven hundredth experiment and we still don't have an answer. We have failed."

"No, my friends," Edison replied, "you haven't failed. It's just that we know more about this subject than anyone else alive. And we're closer to finding the answer, because now we know 700 things not to do." Edison then said, "Don't call it a mistake. Call it an education."

God's Word If anyone knew about mistakes being transformed into glory, it was the apostle Peter. At the most critical time in Jesus' earthly life, Peter denied Him three times. And when Jesus reinstated him, He asked Peter one piercing question three times. "Peter was hurt because Jesus asked him the third time, 'Do you love me?' He said, 'Lord, you know all things; you know that I love you.' Jesus said, 'Feed my sheep' " (John 21:17).

And that's just what Peter did. God later allowed Peter, in spite of his failings, to experience the miracle at Pentecost and establish His church.

Your Walk God has made you in a special way for a specific purpose. And He will transform your failures and flaws into stepping-stones to excellence. As with Edison and Peter, nothing in your past can disqualify you from a future of excellence.

Excellence Is Never Giving Up

Read
2 TIMOTHY 4:1-8

Achievers are not born. They are made. And they are made to endure.

Your World As a teenager, Winston Churchill attended Harrow, a public school in England. He was an average student and a troublemaker. If his father had not been Lord Randolph Churchill, Winston probably would have been expelled.

After Harrow, young Winston attended the university and later entered military service, where he excelled. He was elected prime minister of Britain at age 67. His gifts of leadership and oratory inspired great courage among the British people during World War II.

Years later, the elder statesman spoke to the students of his alma mater, Harrow. The headmaster welcomed Churchill with an effusive introduction. The audience hushed in anticipation. Churchill stepped to the podium and gave this brief speech: "Young men, never give up. Never give up! Never give up! Never, never, never!"

God's Word At the end of his life, the apostle Paul had a similar admonishment to Timothy: "I have fought the good fight, I have finished the race, I have kept the faith" (2 Timothy 4:7).

Your Walk Endurance. It is the key to winning the marathon of life. Personal discipline, vision, optimism, courage, a sense of adventure, a sense of humor, humility, confidence, integrity, and patience all contribute to the pursuit of excellence. But you can't finish the race without endurance. Never give up!

In the Face of Adversity

Read
2 CORINTHIANS 12:1-10

*No success
shines as bright
as the one
surrounded by
the darkness
of disadvantage.*

Your World   Ted Engstrom writes in his book *The Pursuit of Excellence:*

Some of the world's greatest men and women have been saddled with disabilities and adversities but have managed to overcome them.

Cripple him, and you have a Sir Walter Scott.

Lock him in a prison cell, and you have a John Bunyan.

Raise him in abject poverty, and you have an Abraham Lincoln.

Have him or her born black in a society filled with racial discrimination, and you have a Booker T. Washington, a Harriet Tubman, a Marian Anderson, a George Washington Carver, or a Martin Luther King Jr.

Have him born of parents who survived a Nazi concentration camp, paralyze him from the waist down when he is four, and you have an incomparable concert violinist, Itzhak Perlman.

Call him a slow learner, 'retarded,' and write him off as uneducable, and you have an Albert Einstein.

God's Word   Give him a thorn in his flesh, and you have the apostle Paul.

I delight in weaknesses, in insults, in hardships, in persecutions, in difficulties. For when I am weak, then I am strong (2 Corinthians 12:10).

Your Walk   What disadvantage or disability are you using to excuse mediocrity? That is the very thing God will use to transform mediocrity into excellence.

30

"Excellent!"

Read
MATTHEW 25:14-30

Striving for excellence on earth will reap eternal rewards in heaven.

Imagine you are standing in the throne room of heaven. It is Judgment Day. Everyone who has ever lived is standing around you.

It is now your turn to stand before the Judge, Jesus Christ. This is the moment you have dreamed of all your life.

Up close you see the scars from the nails and the thorns. You think about the cross and what Jesus suffered for you and every one of those people standing behind you.

Then you see Jesus looking at you with such love—love you never thought possible during your earthly life. Joy permeates every inch of your resurrected body.

You just know Jesus is about to speak those words, the ones you've been waiting for. The ones your Sunday-school teachers told you about all your life.

But instead, you hear, "Second-rate, mediocre, and wishy-washy servant. Although you were not very faithful in anything, I will put you on 90-day probation to see if you can handle being in charge of even one thing. Nevertheless, come and share your Master's happiness."

Wait a minute! Those aren't the words you're expecting. Isn't being a Christian enough to merit hearing: "Well done [excellent], good and faithful servant!" (Matthew 25:21)?

Your approach to life has eternal consequences. Choose today to live a life of excellence—one that brings honor and glory to God. And one that guarantees blessings now and for eternity.

Striving for excellence on earth will reap eternal rewards in heaven.

*Character
on earth
will prove an
everlasting
possession in the
world to come.*

Character

Making any raw material into a useful and beautiful instrument is the work of a master craftsman. It takes strength, stamina, and determination.

Molding Christian *character* is no easier. Changing our sinful hearts into usable instruments in God's hands requires that He do whatever it takes to bring us into conformity to Jesus Christ.

In your quiet times this week, find out about some of the spiritual disciplines God uses to shape us for His service. Put them into practice, and watch your character being molded into an instrument of God.

God's Righteous Standard

Read
1 PETER 1:13-16

God doesn't wink at unholy character.

Your World In the 1950s, high-school teachers reported that their students' biggest discipline problems were gum-chewing, talking outloud in class, not doing homework, and the like. But today, teachers experience different problems: stabbings, drug use, shootings, and total disregard for authority. What does this deterioration in personal behavior standards reveal? A crisis of character, of moral virtue.

God's Word Our culture has strayed far from God. But as the apostle Peter reveals, God cares deeply about character—especially the character of the people who profess to love Him. "As obedient children, do not conform to the evil desires you had when you lived in ignorance. But just as he who called you is holy, so be holy in all you do; for it is written: 'Be holy, because I am holy' " (1 Peter 1:14-16).

Your Walk God's standard for our behavior remains as high today as it ever was. He required perfect holiness of Adam; He requires the same of all Adam's posterity.

Apart from God's grace, meeting His standard is impossible for us sinful creatures. And even with His grace, we still struggle to develop godly character.

This week's devotions are designed to help you take practical steps to develop character pleasing to God. Ask God to show you areas of personal character weakness. Then ask Him to help you grow in holiness this week.

Character: A Lifelong Struggle

Read
PHILIPPIANS 3:12-16

Nobody ever said living a holy life would be easy.

Your World Jane is driving to work angry, disappointed, and ashamed. Sunday she promised herself that she would start having a consistent, intimate time with God every morning, like she used to. Two days later, she has still failed to act on her resolution.

"What's wrong with me?" she groans to herself while sitting in traffic. "Trying to have a meaningful relationship with God seems hopeless. Maybe I'm not a Christian after all. Maybe I've been fooling myself and everyone else. If I really loved Jesus, how could I be so weak?"

God's Word Jane is right to be dissatisfied with her shallow spiritual life. But what she needs to realize is that building Christian character isn't easy or fast. God has ordained that developing spiritual character should be a complex process, a lifelong struggle, and a lot of hard work. "My dear friends . . . continue to work out your salvation with fear and trembling, for it is God who works in you to will and to act according to his good purpose" (Philippians 2:12-13).

Your Walk In a sense, being a Christian is a lot harder than ignoring God. After all, trying to obey God complicates life significantly. But the price you pay for "[working] out your salvation with fear and trembling" is nothing compared with the reward you receive: a meaningful life of serving God.

The Three Obstacles to Character

Read
JAMES 4:4

Character has powerful enemies; holiness has a more powerful Advocate.

Your World   Reflecting on the difficulties of developing Christian character, Puritan pastor Thomas Watson wrote: "All the danger is when the world gets into the heart. The water is useful for the sailing of the ship; all the danger is when the water gets into the ship; for Christians the fear is when the world gets into the heart. 'Thou shalt not covet.'"

God's Word   According to the Bible, three forces stand in the way of our developing Christian character: the world, the flesh, and the devil.

> Do not love the world or anything in the world. If anyone loves the world, the love of the Father is not in him (1 John 2:15).

> For the sinful nature desires what is contrary to the Spirit, and the Spirit what is contrary to the sinful nature. They are in conflict with each other, so that you do not do what you want (Galatians 5:17).

> Be self-controlled and alert. Your enemy the devil prowls around like a roaring lion looking for someone to devour (1 Peter 5:8).

Your Walk   Character faces formidable enemies. But the power working in you possesses infinitely greater power than any adversary.

Jesus sent the Holy Spirit to help you overcome the odds against character. All you have to do is submit to Him and work in His power, and He will help you overcome even the forces of hell in your quest to grow in holiness.

The Goal of Character

Read
MATTHEW 6:25-34

To develop Christian character, you must put first things first.

Your World The story is told of a captain of a ship who announced to his passengers, "The bad news, ladies and gentlemen, is that we are lost at sea. The good news, however, is that we are making outstanding time!"

The captain ran his ship the way we often run our lives: at high speed but without clear direction.

God's Word Setting goals is vital to accomplishing something with our lives. Likewise, setting a goal is vital to developing Christian character.

Christ sets before us a character goal to reach for, an ideal of virtue to strive to attain: God's righteousness.

> So do not worry, saying, "What shall we eat?" or "What shall we drink?" or "What shall we wear?" For the pagans run after all these things, and your heavenly Father knows that you need them. But seek first his kingdom and his righteousness, and all these things will be given to you as well (Matthew 6:31-33).

Your Walk Like all responsible people, you're concerned about providing your family with the material goods they need. Likewise, you're concerned about providing for the future: your family's education, your retirement, and related issues. But Jesus says that if you will have as your first priority fashioning your character in God's image, He will faithfully provide for your legitimate material concerns.

Character: Love in Action

Read
1 CORINTHIANS 13:1-8

A heart growing in the love of Christ is a life growing in character.

Your World At work Jim takes a lot of heat for his faith. The other people in the office snicker at him when he reads his Bible during lunch. His announcements about a weekly Bible study frequently get removed from the bulletin board. His views on such controversial issues as abortion and the gay-rights movement get a lot of people upset, even though Jim always presents his positions calmly.

Yes, he takes a lot of heat. But he also has the respect of every person he works with. Why? Because he practices what he preaches, and he always treats others with respect and kindness.

In a word, Jim practices love, which is character in action.

God's Word Jim has memorized a passage written by the apostle Paul that details true character. And Jim repeats the passage to himself every day:

> Love is patient, love is kind. It does not envy, it does not boast, it is not proud. It is not rude, it is not self-seeking, it is not easily angered, it keeps no record of wrongs. Love does not delight in evil but rejoices with the truth (1 Corinthians 13:4-6).

Your Walk Be like Jim, and you'll have an impact on your family and community. By developing Christian character, you'll have the strength to stand for truth, regardless of the ridicule of others. And you'll have the strength to do so with love, earning respect and admiration.

Meekness, Not Weakness

Read
MATTHEW 5:5

Meekness is the teachable spirit that allows the strength of the Holy Spirit to flow through.

François de Sales said, "Nothing is so strong as gentleness; nothing so gentle as real strength."

In our day of self-assertiveness (it used to be called "arrogance"), meekness equates with weakness. But according to the Bible, as love is the root of Christian character, meekness (gentleness) is its most basic fruit.

Biblical meekness is

- self-control, not cowardice;
- quiet certainty, not indecision;
- thoughtful patience, not wimpishness.

Far from a designation for only weak types of people, meekness is a quality that describes some of the Bible's most powerful characters. Jesus Himself said, "Come to me, all you who are weary and burdened, and I will give you rest. Take my yoke upon you and learn from me, for I am gentle and humble in heart, and you will find rest for your souls" (Matthew 11:28-29).

As you prepare to worship God this weekend, think about the strengths of your character. Think of some ways you could develop those strengths, then include them on your prayer list.

Also think about the weaknesses of your character. Include these on your prayer list as well. Ask God to bring these traits more into conformity to His Son—the only person with flawless character.

Finally, ask your pastor or a mature Christian friend if he or she will help you develop some ways to measure your progress.

*Faith
reaches out
in trust
to its
Maker.*

What is faith? *Faith* is trust.
Trust in God's promises. Trust in God's Word.
Trust in the way God rules His universe.

In this world, it's sometimes difficult
to have faith. People don't keep their
promises. People direct their lives badly,
and that affects your life.

But in your quiet times this week, look
to God in faith. Unlike anybody
confined to this world, He will
never let you down.

Faith: Trust in God's Promises

Read
HEBREWS 11:1-6

*Have faith
in God,
and He will
be faithful
to you.*

Your World R. Kent Hughes tells the following story to illustrate the meaning of faith:

> [A man] was attempting to cross the frozen St. Lawrence River in Canada. Unsure whether the ice would hold, the man first tested it by laying one hand on it. Then he got down on his knees and gingerly began making his way across. When he got to the middle of the frozen river trembling with fear, he heard a noise behind him. Looking back, to his horror he saw a team of horses pulling a carriage down the road toward the river. And upon reaching the river they didn't stop, but bolted right onto the ice and past him, while he crouched there on all fours, turning a deep crimson.

God's Word Faith is trust. The driver of the carriage had great faith in the strength of the ice; the man crawling had only a little.

God calls His people to put great faith in His holy name: "Some trust in chariots and some in horses, but we trust in the name of the LORD our God" (Psalm 20:7).

Your Walk Trusting God's name means trusting His character, His nature, and His promises on our behalf. This week we'll see what it is to have great faith. And we'll see not only that God deserves our complete trust, but also that He richly rewards His children when we believe in Him with all our hearts.

Righteous-ness Comes by Faith

Read
ROMANS 3:22

*By faith
we are made right
in the sight
of a just and
holy God.*

Your World In an ideal world, God would accept us on the basis of our works. In an ideal world, we would always and thoroughly act for the glory of God and the good of other people. Our motives would never be mixed. We would never usurp God's place in our lives. We would never esteem ourselves above others.

In other words, we would never sin. We would be perfectly righteous. God would have no reason to keep us away from Him.

God's Word But this is not an ideal world. We do sin—heinously. And no sinful person's works are acceptable to God as righteous.

But God satisfied His righteous demands in Christ. And He devised a way to enable us to receive Christ's righteousness apart from our sinful works: the way of faith. "However, to the man who does not work but trusts God who justifies the wicked, his faith is credited as righteousness" (Romans 4:5).

Your Walk *Credited* is a banking term. When Jesus died on the cross, your sins were placed in His account. And when you placed your faith in Him, His righteousness was deposited in your account with God. That transfer is called justification. God sees the faithful "just as if they had never sinned."

Do you believe in Jesus? If so, rejoice! God sees you as righteous because of the righteousness of His Son.

True Faith Produces Obedience

Read
ROMANS 1:5

Justification is by faith— a faith that works.

Your World   The pastor of Trinity Church, shook his head in disappointment and disbelief. He couldn't believe what he was hearing.

John and Tara, two of the young adults of his congregation, had rented an apartment together. They were living in sin.

The pastor visited them, explaining that fornication was still a sin, even though our society believed differently. God wanted them to repent, he said.

John shrugged and chuckled, saying, "Don't worry about it, Pastor. We'll be in heaven. We're just carnal Christians."

God's Word   As we saw yesterday, justification is by faith, not works. But contrary to John and Tara's view, true faith produces good works in a person's life.

The apostle Paul had little patience for the belief that the habitually wicked would inherit the kingdom of heaven:

> Neither the sexually immoral nor idolaters nor adulterers nor male prostitutes nor homosexual offenders . . . will inherit the kingdom of God. And that is what some of you were. But . . . you were justified in the name of the Lord Jesus Christ (1 Corinthians 6:9-11).

Your Walk   As a Christian, you are under God's grace. The law no longer judges you in your standing before God.

But God's law is a divinely inspired guide for your life's walk. And your heart of faith will desire to walk along a pathway pleasing to God.

The Wonder of Faith

Read
JOHN 14:1-13

When faith acts, the world stands back and gasps.

Your World Have you ever had to choose between two options—one alluring, but clearly wrong; the other right, but less attractive?

Faith goes in God's direction, regardless of the consequences. And that kind of faith produces astonishing results.

God's Word Faith works wonders. Trusting in Christ and believing His promises is the divinely ordained way to do God's work in His world.

When we trust God and act, we do God's works. And when our desire is to do God's will, He gives us astonishing power:

> I tell you the truth, anyone who has faith in me will do what I have been doing. He will do even greater things than these, because I am going to the Father. And I will do whatever you ask in my name, so that the Son may bring glory to the Father. You may ask me for anything in my name, and I will do it (John 14:12-14).

Your Walk The results of faithful acts are sometimes difficult to perceive and difficult to understand. But ultimately, those results are always for the best.

Think of some times you have faithfully done God's will—even when doing so was hard. Now think of the results. Can you see how God worked that situation for your good?

Act in faith today by sharing your faith, and God will astonish you with His blessings.

Faith Overcomes the World

Read
MATTHEW 16:13-18

With God on the side of truth, how can it lose?

Your World From the human perspective, truth seems to be taking it on the chin. Many people in today's world are hostile to the idea of absolute truth. What's more, God doesn't exist, they say—or at least He can't be known even if He does exist. And though most households own a Bible, few—pitifully few—know the most elementary facts about Scripture's content.

God's Word From the perspective of the eyes of sight, the Good News seems to be doomed—a casualty of our society's pervasive secularism. But from the perspective of the eyes of faith, the Good News can never be defeated. In fact, even in these troubled times, we can be sure of this: God's truth will win.

> This is love for God: to obey his commands. And his commands are not burdensome, for everyone born of God overcomes the world. This is the victory that has overcome the world, even our faith (1 John 5:3-4).

Your Walk Neither the world, the devil, nor the sin within our own hearts can stand up to true faith—the kind of faith that produces obedience to God's commands.

The next time you're discouraged by what you read in the newspapers, set your mind on Christ. Remember His love for you and His promise: He will overcome the world.

The Reward

Read
MATTHEW 25:14-23

The smallest seed of faith will grow with cultivation.

Let's face it: Life is a struggle. Financially, relationally, emotionally, spiritually—sometimes life seems mainly a series of problems to be overcome, battles to be waged, trials to be endured.

Yes, the Christian life is a struggle. But that isn't the whole story. It's also a great and joyous exercise in faithful overcoming.

By faith we assault the problems that beset us. By faith we defend ourselves against the devil's schemes. By faith we believe that Jesus' life is being lived out in us. By faith we trust His commands are good for us. And by faith we trust this encouraging promise: The faithful will one day receive a glorious reward. "He who overcomes will, like them, be dressed in white. I will never blot out his name from the book of life, but will acknowledge his name before my Father and his angels" (Revelation 3:5).

Our faith presently overcomes sin's penalty, and, to a degree, sin's power. But sin's power won't be fully eradicated until that day when Christ returns, giving us new and sinless bodies.

And on the day when sin is banished from the new heavens and new earth, we will hear Christ acknowledging us before His Father in the most beautiful words ever spoken: "Come, you who are blessed by my Father; take your inheritance, the kingdom prepared for you since the creation of the world" (Matthew 25:34).

*True charity
comes from—
and honors—
God.*

Charity

When most people hear the word *charity*, they picture somebody doing good deeds for people in need. But charity is more than good deeds. It's the heart attitude out of which good deeds flow. And because sin has spoiled our hearts, true charity depends on the grace of God changing a person's heart through the Holy Spirit.

Find out more about charity in your quiet times this week. And practice Spirit-driven charity in your life.

Un-Conditional Love in Action

Read
1 CORINTHIANS 13

*When the heart
is filled
with charity,
loving action
always follows.*

Your World When we think of the word *charity*, we usually think of giving. But charity is more than that—much more. Charity is the condition of the heart—the virtue—out of which flows all charitable action.

Charity is unconditional love for God, and unconditional love for ourselves and our neighbors out of love for God. No wonder theologians have called charity the greatest of all virtues.

God's Word But like all virtues, charity isn't dormant; it acts. In 1 Corinthians 13, the apostle Paul reveals to us how a person with charity, or unconditional love, acts:

> Though I bestow all my goods to feed the poor, and though I give my body to be burned, and have not charity, it profiteth me nothing. Charity suffereth long, and is kind; charity envieth not; charity vaunteth not itself, is not puffed up, doth not behave itself unseemly, seeketh not her own, is not easily provoked, thinketh no evil (1 Corinthians 13:3-5 KJV).

Your Walk Here's a good project for your quiet times this week: Memorize the above passage. Use a modern translation, if you prefer.

David hid the Scriptures in his heart so that he wouldn't sin against God (Psalm 119:11). Hide God's words about unconditional love in your heart. Cultivate the virtue of charity in your own life, and you will be more likely to give love in the name of Him who has loved you so charitably.

Charity Gives Freely

Read
LUKE 10:25-37

Charity doesn't make those in need prove their need.

Your World Jesus demanded nothing from a man with leprosy before curing him of his disease.

Mother Teresa demanded nothing from the untouchables of Calcutta before giving them food, care, rest, and love.

Charity demands nothing before fulfilling the needs of the downcast. Charity gives freely, happily, and without condition.

God's Word In the parable of the Good Samaritan, Jesus illustrates that charity asks no questions before doing good.

When a man was attacked by robbers, a priest and a Levite, considering the man unworthy of their time, ignored him. But a Samaritan acted with charity.

> A Samaritan, as he traveled, came where the man was; and when he saw him, he took pity on him. He went to him and bandaged his wounds, pouring on oil and wine. Then he put the man on his own donkey, took him to an inn and took care of him (Luke 10:33-34).

Jesus' conclusion? "Go and do likewise" (verse 37).

Your Walk You can "go and do likewise" in a number of ways. There are numerous nonprofit organizations that exist specifically to give charitably to those in need. Contact one of these organizations and give of your time, money, or other resources.

Pour oil and wine on the wounds of someone in need, and God will pour His blessings upon you.

Sometimes Charity Must Be Tough

Read
2 THESSALONIANS
3:6-10

Tough charity protects the lazy from themselves.

Your World   The Salvation Army is one of the country's largest and most respected charitable organizations. And through its many programs, the Salvation Army gives unconditionally to the needy, without asking questions.

But the Salvation Army knows human nature. That's why it sometimes practices tough charity. Yes, the Salvation Army will house and feed people on an ongoing basis if they work responsibly in its adult rehabilitation centers, thereby helping the Salvation Army mission and learning a trade.

As a result, the long-term poor are given what they most need: a chance to learn the kind of responsibility that will enable them to help themselves.

God's Word   Charity does what's best for others. And so sometimes charity must be tough. When someone repeatedly uses charity to excuse laziness, charity must eventually say no:

> In the name of the Lord Jesus Christ, we command you, brothers, to keep away from every brother who is idle. . . . For even when we were with you, we gave you this rule: "If a man will not work, he shall not eat" (2 Thessalonians 3:6,10).

Your Walk   To some people, charity means never saying no to the needy. To others, charity is actually considered an evil because they feel you should never say yes to those in need.

Follow the Scriptures. Avoid the two extremes by striking the biblical balance: Give initially without condition; wisely practice tough charity over the long term.

The Charitable Imitate God

Read
MATTHEW 5:43-48

*Be charitable
to others
as your
heavenly Father
has been
charitable to you.*

Your World   The ethic of the Bible can be summed up in one word: *imitation.* According to J. I. Packer, imitating God is the number one principle of behavior for a member of God's family.

Commenting on Jesus' statement "Be perfect, therefore, as your heavenly Father is perfect" (Matthew 5:48), Dr. Packer wrote: "The children [of God] must show the family likeness in their conduct. Jesus is here spelling out 'Be ye holy, for I am holy'—and spelling it out in family terms."

God's Word   God is the supreme standard of virtue. God's character is virtue, and we are virtuous only to the degree we imitate Him.

And the biblical message is clear: God is a God of charity to all. Not one person on earth is completely shut off from His gifts:

> You have heard that it was said, "Love your neighbor and hate your enemy." But I tell you: Love your enemies and pray for those who persecute you, that you may be sons of your Father in heaven. He causes his sun to rise on the evil and the good, and sends rain on the righteous and the unrighteous (Matthew 5:43-46).

Your Walk   Your heavenly Father is charitable to all—even to those who reject Him. Is there a person at work or in church who has rejected you? Offer that person an act of kindness. Imitate your Father's charity, and He will be faithful to richly bless you.

The Charity of Believers

Read
2 CORINTHIANS 9:6-9

Without Christian charity, the world would be a much crueler place.

Your World Have you ever wondered why the names of hospitals so commonly include words such as *Presbyterian, Baptist, Methodist, Adventist, or Saint*? Have you ever wondered why soup kitchens and other charities to the poor are so often located in the basements of churches?

The reason is clear: When Christians follow the example of their Master, they give. They give a lot. Most of the charitable institutions spawned during the Industrial Revolution—hospitals, clinics, secondhand clothing organizations—were Christian in origin and mission.

God's Word The believers who give money, time, and effort to establish charitable organizations are following the example of the Macedonian churches' charity:

> And now, brothers, we want you to know about the grace that God has given the Macedonian churches. Out of the most severe trial, their overflowing joy and their extreme poverty welled up in rich generosity. For I testify that they gave as much as they were able, and even beyond their ability (2 Corinthians 8:1-3).

Your Walk Are you giving as much as you are able to God's cause on earth? Examine your budget. If giving is a priority, you'll see it in your check register. If giving is not a priority, perhaps your motives need an adjustment. God will faithfully reward sacrifices made in obedience to Him and for the benefit of others.

The Better Way

Read
1 CORINTHIANS 7:29-31

Every charitable act is a stepping-stone toward heaven.

Charity isn't easy. In fact, for sinful human beings, true charity is impossible. Charity lays aside all considerations of personal gain—something we can't do apart from God.

Charity is incompatible with the spirit of selfish consumption that pervades much of our consumer-oriented society. That's not to say material blessings are evil. But an inordinate affection for things cannot coexist with a spirit of true charity.

As believers, we must walk in the paths illuminated for us by God's Word. If we are to cultivate the virtue of charity, we must turn away from crassly seeking without restraint an endless increase of personal possessions and benefits.

Instead there is a better way: We must embrace a greater desire for the glory of God and the good of other people. And we must act on that desire in our daily lives.

As the apostle Paul wrote, "What I mean, brothers, is that the time is short. From now on . . . those who use the things of the world [should live] as if not engrossed in them. For this world in its present form is passing away" (1 Corinthians 7:29, 31).

Life is fleeting. There is a lot to be done in this world to prepare for the next. God calls us to lay up eternal treasure through charity. But many of us spend our lives selfishly building treasures that will decay.

There is still time to change. And God is ready to forgive, forget, renew, and empower us with His charity, His help, and His love.

Confidence

It's no wonder people are neurotic.
That which humans desire most—fellowship
with God—was ruined at the Fall. While deeply
desiring God, we furiously flee from Him.
Our souls live insecurely in the tension.
Enter Christ.

By reconciling us with God, our Savior gives us
new reason for *confidence*. And by promising
even greater fellowship with the Father one
day, Jesus fills us with joy inexpressible and
the confidence spawned by hope.

Don't view life with fear. Stand up and shout!
Christ died for you. That's good enough for
God; it ought to be good enough for you.

Confidence Lost

Read
GENESIS 3:1-10

Christ's love breaks the chains of sin and insecurity.

Your World   "I can't believe it," a young woman wrote in a letter to her college roommate.

"I waited for weeks to meet my favorite mystery writer at a book-signing party. After standing in line for 40 minutes, I was face-to-face with her. Suddenly I was a basket case. Instead of intelligently telling her how much her work has meant to me, I babbled something incoherent and shoved my book in her face. She must have thought I was a blithering idiot."

God's Word   The young woman shouldn't be too ashamed. Confidence can be fleeting in this world.

There was a time when the human race exuded a natural confidence—even in the presence of God. But the Fall destroyed that confidence. When Adam and Eve sinned, they felt the terrible insecurity of a sinful nature.

> The man and his wife heard the sound of the LORD God as he was walking in the garden in the cool of the day, and they hid from the LORD God among the trees of the garden. But the LORD God called to the man, "Where are you?" He answered, "I heard you in the garden, and I was afraid" (Genesis 3:8-10).

Your Walk   Do you experience feelings of insecurity? Do your circumstances cause you to fear? Don't worry. It's understandable. But as you'll discover this week, there is plenty of reason to be confident in Christ. And with God's help, your feelings will follow what your reason discovers.

Is Confidence the Same as Pride?

Read
2 CHRONICLES 32:1-21

The line between confidence and pride may be razor-thin, but it's canyon-deep.

Your World   Of pride, C. S. Lewis wrote: "There is no fault which makes a man more unpopular, and no fault which we are more unconscious of in ourselves. And the more we have it ourselves, the more we dislike it in others."

There must be a distinction between pride and confidence then, for confidence is a feature we admire. Here's the difference: True confidence is rooted in trusting God and His works; pride, or false confidence, is rooted in an inordinate trust in oneself.

God's Word   When the forces of Sennacherib, king of Assyria, laid siege to Jerusalem, King Hezekiah displayed godly confidence: "Be strong and courageous. Do not be afraid or discouraged because of the king of Assyria and the vast army with him, for there is a greater power with us than with him" (2 Chronicles 32:7).

Sennacherib, on the other hand, boasted pridefully, blaspheming God: "[No] god of any nation or kingdom has been able to deliver his people from my hand or the hand of my fathers. How much less will your god deliver you from my hand!" (verse 15).

Your Walk   Hezekiah's confidence was contagious: "The people gained confidence from what Hezekiah the king of Judah said" (verse 8).

Put your trust in God, and walk confidently as a result. Your confidence will be contagious, too.

Encouragement Builds Confidence

Read
PHILIPPIANS 1:3-6

*Encouragement
is the key
to confidence.*

Your World Encouragement is to confidence what a spring shower is to a garden.

Encouragement refreshes our hearts. We are reminded that we are here for a purpose; we are important; we are needed.

Encouragement nourishes our souls. When we are encouraged, our most inner selves feel renewed.

Encouragement bears fruit in our lives. When other people tell us they appreciate something we have done, we do it with greater confidence the next time.

God's Word The apostle Paul knew the power of encouragement. Paul had great confidence in God. So he greatly encouraged the Christians at Philippi, reminding them that God loved them, was at work in them, and would continue to bless them.

> In all my prayers for all of you, I always pray with joy because of your partnership in the gospel from the first day until now, being confident of this, that he who began a good work in you will carry it on to completion until the day of Christ Jesus (Philippians 1:4-6).

Your Walk Think of a person in your life who lacks confidence. Perhaps all he or she needs is a little encouragement.

Make a difference in that person's life. Refresh his heart; nourish his soul; cultivate fruit in his life. Be like the apostle Paul. Build a believer's confidence by being an encourager.

Confident Before the Face of God

Read
EPHESIANS 3:12

Christ's sacrifice is the Christian's confidence.

Your World Imagine you're an Old Testament priest. A man approaches you with a sin to confess and an animal to kill. He puts his hands on the animal and cuts its throat. You drain the blood, sprinkling some of it in front of the curtain in the sanctuary. You remove some organs from the animal and burn them on the altar. You then take what remains of the carcass and burn it outside the camp in a chosen place.

And your day has just begun.

God's Word Fortunately, we don't have to perform such sacrifices. We can feel confident approaching our Father without having to offer an animal to atone for our sins.

That's because Jesus Christ offered Himself for us, and His blood forever cleanses us from sin. Therefore, God encourages us to come before Him boldly through prayer:

> Since we have a great high priest who has gone through the heavens, Jesus the Son of God . . . let us then approach the throne of grace with confidence, so that we may receive mercy and find grace to help us in our time of need (Hebrews 4:14,16).

Your Walk Access to the throne room of God through prayer is, for some, an unclaimed blessing. If you struggle with prayer, keep in mind the value of Christ's sacrifice. You can approach the throne of grace with confidence because, in Christ, God sees you as if you had never sinned.

Confidence in Our Protector

Read
PSALM 32:7

*When God
is for us,
who can be
against us?*

Your World Tornadoes, hurricanes, typhoons, floods—each of these natural disasters wreaks havoc in people's lives. But many who have experienced major earthquakes describe a feeling perhaps unique among survivors of catastrophes. When the ground begins to shake, a sensation of intense vertigo becomes overwhelming. Put off balance both physically and emotionally, some earthquake victims don't regain their confidence for months, even years.

God's Word In an earthquake, the ground can't be trusted. But God can always be trusted.

Faith is solid ground for our souls. Being assured that whatever happens is from the hand of a loving Father breeds rock-like confidence, even in the face of severe trials. Or, as Stephen found, even in the face of losing it all:

> "Look," [Stephen] said, "I see heaven open and the Son of Man standing at the right hand of God." At this they covered their ears and, yelling at the top of their voices, they all rushed at him, dragged him out of the city and began to stone him. . . . While they were stoning him, Stephen prayed, "Lord Jesus, receive my spirit" (Acts 7:56-59).

Your Walk Look up the word *protect* in a Bible concordance. Take some time this weekend to memorize a verse about God's protection of His people. Whenever you feel insecure because of life's trials, stand on the truth of that verse—with confidence.

Godly Confidence

Read
PSALM 17:14-15

Our confidence is rooted in the character of God, who keeps His covenants and never breaks His promises.

As we've seen in our readings so far, confidence was lost at the Fall; it was regained in principle on the cross. But because we haven't yet received all that Christ purchased on the cross, we still struggle with insecurity. But a time is coming when that struggle will be over.

When Christ returns, when He raises us from the dead, when He changes those of us who are still alive, the battle will be fully won. Our hearts will be sinless. We will always choose to do good. Being unencumbered by sin, we will be filled with awe but empty of fear as we walk with God.

> God is love. Whoever lives in love lives in God, and God in him. In this way, love is made complete among us so that we will have confidence on the day of judgment, because in this world we are like him. There is no fear in love. But perfect love drives out fear (1 John 4:16-18).

No fear. Just total confidence. That godly confidence won't be devilish pride. We won't regard ourselves as the center of our lives. Instead, we'll be secure in the loving presence of God. And we'll be filled with joy at the prospect of serving Him forever.

Experience the firstfruits of that confidence this weekend. Lift up your heart in worship to the God who bought your confidence on the cross, and who will one day return to give you the full benefits of the confidence you now only begin to feel.

*Wisdom
is seeing life—
and living it—
from God's
point of view.*

Wisdom

All of us in today's fast-paced society have problems. And we're not above seeking help. But the help we need is practical help.

Few of us have time for theoretical discussions about esoteric topics. Instead, we seek advice we can use. Suggestions we can implement in our lives. Counsel that comes from experience. In other words, we seek *wisdom*.

In your quiet times this week, discover that the Bible is intensely practical. And apply its wisdom in your own life.

From Your Mind to Your Feet

Read
GALATIANS 5:25

Wisdom isn't wisdom until it travels from your mind through your heart to your feet.

Your World   According to the *Random House Dictionary of the English Language,* wisdom is "knowledge of what is true or right coupled with just judgment as to action."

Notice the two elements in the definition: knowledge of the truth, and acting on that knowledge. Knowing the truth and applying the truth—that's wisdom. That's skillful Christian living.

God's Word   God wants us to know the truth about Him. But He isn't satisfied if our knowledge isn't applied to our lives. He wants us to regard both knowledge and its application as part of a lifelong, passionate pursuit.

> Blessed is the man who finds wisdom, the man who gains understanding, for she is more profitable than silver and yields better returns than gold. She is more precious than rubies; nothing you desire can compare with her (Proverbs 3:13-15).

Your Walk   To help us to live skillfully, to show us how to apply His truth in our experience, God has graciously given us the Book of Proverbs. As you have your devotional times, meditate on the truths you'll learn from the wise sayings of Solomon and others.

But don't stop there. Let the meditations of your mind sink down into the recesses of your heart. And then walk according to the truths God reveals to you in His Word.

Wisdom Has Its Rewards

Read
GALATIANS 6:7

Wise living is the best prescription against financial ruin.

Your World In his book *Man in the Mirror*, Patrick M. Morley says there are three ways that Christians look at money: 1) as a necessary evil, 2) as a necessary reward for those who buy God's favor with a tithe, and 3) as a trust given by God in varying proportions to faithful stewards.

The biblical view, of course, is number 3. Yes, God abundantly blesses wise, faithful living. No, God doesn't become a debtor to His people when they give to advance His cause.

God's Word God doesn't promise to make Christians rich. Nor does He forbid believers from making money. But He does promise that those who wisely handle the resources He entrusts to them will have all they need in this world.

> Long life is in [wisdom's] right hand; in her left hand are riches and honor (Proverbs 3:16).

> A faithful man will be richly blessed, but one eager to get rich will not go unpunished (Proverbs 28:20).

Your Walk Walk Thru the Bible Ministries offers an outstanding resource to help you handle your finances with wisdom. *The Master Your Money Video Series* is filled with practical advice about being a good steward of your finances.

Ask your pastor to make this series a part of your church library. Watch it with your Sunday-school class or in your home with your spouse, and then apply its truths to your life.

The Answer to Conflict

Read
PSALM 29:11

As surely as foolishness leads to conflict, wisdom leads to peace.

Your World   Peace. It's one of the world's most sought-after commodities. Nations seek peace with other nations; political parties seek peace with rival parties; husbands seek peace with wives; children seek peace with parents; employees seek peace with employers; and on and on it goes.

But as much as peace is desired, it is elusive. Peace is hard to come by in a sinful world made up of selfish individuals.

God's Word   But God hasn't left us without guidance toward achieving peace. He has revealed the way to peace: the way of wisdom.

People who act wisely, who live life skillfully, who apply God's truth in their lives, will be rewarded with peace.

> [Wisdom's] ways are pleasant ways, and all her paths are peace (Proverbs 3:17).

> When a man's ways are pleasing to the LORD, he makes even his enemies live at peace with him (Proverbs 16:7).

Your Walk   Are you experiencing conflict with a member of your family? Someone at work? Someone at church? God's Word will show you the way to live with other people. God's Holy Spirit will enable you to follow that way.

Ask your pastor to show you which passages teach God's wisdom about the kind of relationship you're struggling with. Then ask God's Spirit to help you act according to the wisdom He reveals in His Word.

Long Life and Joyous Blessing

Read
PROVERBS 23:19

*It is wise
to take care
of our bodies,
the Holy Spirit's
temple.*

Your World   The statistics are in and the verdict is clear: People who wisely regard physical health as a priority live longer than people who treat their bodies carelessly.

On average, those who don't smoke, don't abuse alcoholic beverages, avoid sugar and caffeine, eat high-fiber and low-fat foods, and exercise regularly live up to ten years longer than those who have poor health habits.

God's Word   That shouldn't come as a surprise. After all, God says in His Word that taking care of the body He gave you is wisdom. And He rewards those who live wisely with longevity and good health.

> Do you not know that your body is a temple of the Holy Spirit, who is in you, whom you have received from God? . . . Therefore honor God with your body (1 Corinthians 6:19-20).

Your Walk   The Book of Proverbs is made up of general principles, rather than particular promises. It would be a mistake to suppose that when a proverb says the wise will live long lives, there are no exceptions to that rule.

Wisdom is more like common sense. Though there are exceptions, living wisely generally brings blessing; living foolishly generally brings only misery. Here's a wise, commonsense judgment: If you take care of your body, your body will take care of you for a long time.

Learning Wisdom from the Wise

Read
PROVERBS 2:20

To become wise, surround yourself with wisdom.

Your World Dutch artists of the Reformation era who wanted to paint like Rembrandt sought to learn from the master himself. Musicians who wanted to play the organ or compose like J. S. Bach joined his music school. Lawyers who want to learn from a particular Supreme Court justice seek to become one of that justice's law clerks. And graduate students who want to learn from a particular academic seek to become one of his or her Ph.D. candidates.

God's Word Students learn from masters. That's true in the worlds of art, music, law, and education. It's also true in the area of wise living:

> He who walks with the wise grows wise, but a companion of fools suffers harm (Proverbs 13:20).

> A righteous man is cautious in friendship, but the way of the wicked leads them astray (Proverbs 12:26).

Your Walk Wisdom can best be learned from the wise. Conversely, of course, foolishness is learned from the foolish.

Because we learn from those we are around, you should be discerning in your relationships. Seek to establish regular, long-term relationships with people who show wisdom in their life choices. Spend time with people who live according to God's Word, and their wisdom will rub off on you.

God's Perspective

Read
JOB 28:20-28

God knows all things, so to achieve wisdom, we must live according to His Word.

When Job underwent his suffering, he had time to reflect on his condition. He knew he was a righteous man, yet he was suffering a terrible calamity. He knew he had lived wisely, yet his life was in complete turmoil.

You can almost hear the anguish in Job's voice as he pleads, "Where then does wisdom come from? Where does understanding dwell?" (Job 28:20).

Then Job has a profound insight: To know true wisdom, we have to look at things from God's perspective. For by ourselves, we know only our own experience. But God knows everything, including His reasons for doing things we don't understand: "God understands the way to [wisdom] and he alone knows where it dwells, for he views the ends of the earth and sees everything under the heavens" (verses 23-24).

Job's reflection led him to a simple conclusion—simple, yet utterly profound. Those who want to live wisely in this world must live according to the rules established by Him who made the world: "The fear of the Lord—that is wisdom, and to shun evil is understanding" (verses 28).

In the Creator's universe, playing by His rules is wisdom. That makes sense, doesn't it? Live by that commonsense truth, and your life will be productive and fulfilling. The all-wise and all-knowing God of love will richly bless you—in this world and especially in the world to come.

Life's Challenges

*Happiness
is where
you find it
and very seldom
where you
seek it.*

Happiness

According to the world, *happiness* stems from money, fame, and power. But real happiness comes only through Jesus Christ. In Him we find unconditional love, unconditional acceptance, and meaning and purpose in life, regardless of our age or circumstances.

Life is too short to miss the real thing. Discover more about happiness in your quiet times this week.

He Who Would Be Happy

Read
PSALM 1

Obedience, far from restricting happiness, nourishes and matures it.

Your World Hardly anybody would disagree with the idea that everybody wants to be happy. But a lot of people have different views about how to attain that goal.

Some seek happiness in work, others in play; some even seek happiness in alcohol and drugs. The problem is that people often look for happiness on their own terms because they do not understand the true path to happiness.

God's Word Because God wants His people to be happy, He has revealed to us in His Word and world the way to happiness. "Blessed [happy] is the man who does not walk in the counsel of the wicked or stand in the way of sinners or sit in the seat of mockers. But his delight is in the law of the LORD, and on his law he meditates day and night" (Psalm 1:1-2).

In other words, the way to happiness—true happiness—is obedience.

Your Walk Try as you might, you can't dictate to God your own route to happiness and then expect Him to submit to your judgment. As a matter of fact, to pursue happiness in a way that God has forbidden is to guarantee unhappiness.

To play a board game successfully, you have to play by the rules. So it is in the game of life. Live by God's rules, and you'll have this promise to claim: Whatever you do will prosper (Psalm 1:3).

The Serious Business of Happiness

Read
ACTS 5:41

*Happy
is the person
who takes life
seriously enough
to have a
truly good time.*

Your World   G. K. Chesterton, the brilliant English author of the early twentieth century, wrote:

> Happiness is as grave and practical as sorrow, if not more so. We might as well imagine that a man could carve a cardboard chicken or live on imitation loaves of bread, as suppose that any man could get happiness out of things that are merely light or laughable.

God's Word   Chesterton's point is one of life's more interesting ironies: Happiness isn't frivolous; it's serious business. Jesus taught the same paradox in the Beatitudes:

> Blessed are the poor in spirit, for theirs is the kingdom of heaven. Blessed are those who mourn, for they will be comforted. . . . Blessed are those who hunger and thirst for righteousness, for they will be filled (Matthew 5:3-4, 6).

Some versions of the Bible use the word *happy* instead of *blessed*. Happiness doesn't come from frivolity and indulgence as we might expect, but from humility, self-sacrifice, concern for other people—in short, righteousness.

Your Walk   Does that mean you can't have any fun? Certainly not! But it does mean you'll have more fun than you ever imagined if your relationship with God is what it should be.

Do you hunger and thirst for happiness? Then hunger and thirst for righteousness. Read God's Word and do what it says. You *will* be satisfied.

One Big, Happy Family

Read
EPHESIANS 5:22-33

Without God, family happiness is impossible. With God, all things are possible.

Your World Benjamin Disraeli, British prime minister from 1874 to 1880, obtained a huge fortune when he married a wealthy widow 12 years his senior. Their marriage was very happy.

Toward the end of his life, Disraeli would joke with his wife, saying that he only married her for her money. His wife, unaffected by such joking, would say, "But if you had to do it again, you'd do it for love."

God's Word God designed the family to be a place of peace, security, and harmony in our lives:

> Blessed are all who fear the LORD, who walk in his ways. . . . Your wife will be like a fruitful vine within your house; your sons will be like olive shoots around your table. Thus is the man blessed who fears the LORD (Psalm 128:1, 3-4).

Your Walk Divorce, domestic violence, adultery, and teen suicide are widespread. And being a Christian is no guarantee of escaping a family crisis. Christians divorce almost as often as non-Christians.

What's the solution? How can you find and keep the happiness of domestic tranquillity? You can follow God's Word in your family relationships.

Are you a husband? Love your wife. A wife? Respect your husband. These simple commands require creativity and commitment. And you'll never obey them perfectly. But if you want to, God the Holy Spirit will help you grow in familial graces.

Heigh-Ho, Heigh-Ho, It's Off to Work We Go

Read
ECCLESIASTES 10:18

The work that's best for the world is the work to which you've been called.

Your World In his book *Leisure and Work*, sociologist Stanley Parker wrote, "Research in the various social sciences shows that both work and leisure are necessary to a healthy life and a healthy society."

God's Word Work has been around for a long time—since the Garden of Eden. In fact, God ordained work before sin ever entered the picture. And from the beginning, work has been an important part of a happy life: "God blessed [Adam and Eve] and said to them, 'Be fruitful and increase in number; fill the earth and subdue it' " (Genesis 1:28).

How were our first parents to accomplish the subduing part of this task? "The LORD God took the man and put him in the Garden of Eden to work it and take care of it" (Genesis 2:15).

Your Walk Work, originally a blessing, was tainted by the Fall. Work is now both fulfilling and exasperating, both blessing and curse.

But take comfort in this: Regardless of the kind of work you do (assuming, of course, that it isn't illegal or immoral), your work is fulfilling a purpose in God's world. Why? Because all work—even seemingly menial work—is a part of God's work of subduing the earth.

Begin to see your work as part of God's plan, and it will promote, rather than prevent, your health and happiness.

The Happiness of Loyalty

Read
1 PETER 2:17

The world says, "Be loyal to yourself." Jesus says, "Be loyal to Me."

Your World   Charles Colson was special counsel to President Richard M. Nixon before the Watergate scandal forced the president out of the White House and Mr. Colson into prison.

Mr. Colson recounts lecturing at a college after his release. During the question-and-answer period, one student asked Mr. Colson how he could have remained loyal to Nixon. Colson replied, "Because he was my friend."

The audience burst into applause.

God's Word   Colson's courageous loyalty struck an emotional chord—even in an audience unsympathetic to the politics of Richard Nixon.

Jesus wants that same kind of loyalty—even in the most trying circumstances:

> Blessed are you when people insult you, persecute you and falsely say all kinds of evil against you because of me. Rejoice and be glad, because great is your reward in heaven (Matthew 5:11-12).

Your Walk   Are you loyal to Christ? Do you take advantage of opportunities God gives you to speak about His Son? Or do you let such occasions slip away for fear of being ridiculed?

To trust Jesus even in the face of ridicule is to be happy, glad, rewarded. When you are loyal to Christ, you receive a double blessing: You share the good news of God's saving love, and you contribute to your own happiness—even if some people make fun of you.

What Is Happiness?

Read
MATTHEW 5:1-12

*No one
can be happy
apart from God.*

In his book *Finding Happiness in the Most Unlikely Places,* Donald W. McCullough points out that it's easier to say what happiness isn't than to say what it is. Mr. McCullough writes that happiness is not

- feeling satisfied with oneself (Jesus blessed the poor in spirit);
- feeling cheerful (Jesus blessed the mourners);
- feeling powerful (Jesus blessed the meek);
- feeling fulfilled (Jesus blessed those who hunger and thirst for righteousness);
- feeling detached from human suffering (Jesus blessed the merciful);
- feeling free to choose any option (Jesus blessed the pure in heart);
- feeling delivered from stress and tension (Jesus blessed the peacemakers);
- feeling accepted by the world (Jesus blessed those whom the world did not accept because of their faith in Him).

In other words, happiness is not a feeling. Then what is it?

Happiness is a state of mind that stems from a right relationship with God. True happiness, then, is strong enough to experience both pleasant and unpleasant feelings.

Earlier we said that everybody wants happiness. But rather than being the goal of life, happiness is the state of mind that results from achieving the real goal: communion with God.

*To master
temptation,
let Christ
master you.*

Temptation

Let's face it:
Life is full of *temptations*.
The world entices us at every moment from
every corner. And if that isn't bad enough,
we struggle with evil inclinations within our
own hearts. But that's not even the worst of it.
Satan and his demonic followers know our
weaknesses and set traps for believers
at every turn.

But we don't have to succumb.
As believers we have the power to resist.
The Holy Spirit is more powerful than
the world, the sinful nature, and the devil.
Find out how to flee from temptation
in your quiet times this week.

Satan's Temptation: Trust Me

Read
MATTHEW 6:9-15

*The father
of lies
can never
be trusted.*

Your World *Trust.* Reduced to its essence, the message of the entire Bible can be summed up in two words: *Trust God.*

But God isn't the only supernatural being who wants your trust. Satan wants it, too. Though he tempts different people in different ways, all his temptations are essentially the same: crafty appeals for trust.

"Trust me," he says. "Trust that I can make you happy. Don't trust God. He just wants to keep you from having the things— and the fun—that you want."

God's Word Satan tempted our first parents by undermining their trust in their Creator and asking them to trust him instead. The devil's strategy was all too successful:

> Now the serpent was more crafty than any of the wild animals the LORD God had made. He said to the woman, "Did God really say, 'You must not eat from any tree in the garden'? . . . You will not surely die. . . . For God knows that when you eat of [the tree in the middle of the garden] your eyes will be opened, and you will be like God, knowing good and evil" (Genesis 3:1, 4-5).

Your Walk Whenever you experience temptation, say to yourself, "This is an issue of trust. Whom do I trust: Satan or God?" In such times, stand on the promises of God. Trust Him, regardless of the temptation, and Satan and his tempting power will flee.

Strength Takes Time— and Prayer

Read
EPHESIANS 6:10-18

To resist temptation, put on your spiritual armor.

Your World When James Garfield was president of the United States, he recounted an event that happened when he was president of Hiram College.

A man asked Garfield to shorten the curriculum for his son. "My son wants to graduate quickly," the father said. "Can you arrange it?"

"It depends on what you want to make of him," Garfield replied. "God takes centuries to make an oak. But He only takes two months to make a squash."

Building spiritual strength—the kind able to withstand the devil's tricks—is like building a strong oak. It takes time.

God's Word We live in a world of instant gratification. Believers tend to want instant spiritual growth. But the time-tested, biblical method of resisting temptation is through diligent use of the means of grace—especially prayer and God's Word. Paul wrote to the Ephesian church,

> Be strong in the Lord and in his mighty power. Put on the full armor of God so that you can take your stand against the devil's schemes. . . . Take the helmet of salvation and the sword of the Spirit, which is the word of God. And pray in the Spirit on all occasions with all kinds of prayers and requests (Ephesians 6:10-11, 17-18).

Your Walk Do you want to resist temptation? Of course you do, or you wouldn't be reading this. Ask God daily to give you strength, and He will answer your prayers.

Temptation Is Serious Business

Read
LUKE 8:1-15

*Temptation
can be deadly
to a person's soul.*

Your World James listened intently as Larry, the student leader of his dorm, talked about Christ. He knew Larry's words were true. He sensed the weight of his own sin. He responded to Larry's invitation to invite Christ into his life.

That was last week. This evening James feels quite different. He looks out his door to make sure Larry isn't around. Then he slips out of the dorm and heads to a wild fraternity party. "I can't stand the thought of people calling me a religious nut like Larry," James rationalizes to himself.

God's Word Temptation isn't something to be taken lightly. It's the devil's tool, and he is a powerful enemy. In fact, as Jesus explains in the parable of the sower, sometimes Satan's temptation is powerful enough to draw those with weak faith away from the truth:

> A sower went out to sow his seed. And as he sowed . . . some fell on rock; and as soon as it sprang up, it withered away because it lacked moisture. . . . The ones on the rock are those who, when they hear, receive the word with joy; and these have no root, who believe for a while and in time of temptation fall away (Luke 8:5-6,13 NKJV).

Your Walk Never regard temptation lightly. Keep your faith alive by keeping yourself in God's Word, in prayer, and in fellowship with other believers. Sink deep spiritual roots, and temptation won't draw you away from Christ.

God Provides the Escape Route

Read
1 CORINTHIANS 10:6-13

The voice of conscience can never be completely silenced.

Your World Ellen knew she was sinning. With every step she took toward his hotel room, a voice told her to stop, turn back, and run to safety.

Like thousands of other college freshmen, Ellen went to Daytona Beach for spring break. And like many, Ellen got caught up in the wildness, eventually acting foolishly in a Daytona Beach hotel room.

Now Ellen is miserable. She sinned. She knows it. And as a believer, Ellen knows she could have avoided sinning. She could have listened to God, rather than the spirit of the world at work all around her.

God's Word Believers don't ever have to sin. God is always watching out for us, providing a way of escape during times of temptation.

As the apostle Paul wrote,

> If you think you are standing firm, be careful that you don't fall! No temptation has seized you except what is common to man. And God is faithful; he will not let you be tempted beyond what you can bear. But when you are tempted, he will also provide a way out so that you can stand up under it (1 Corinthians 10:12-13).

Your Walk Do you lose patience with your children? Look for the way to quiet your heart. Do you fail to mention Christ to unbelieving friends? Look for the opportunity to give Him honor.

Whatever your area of sin, look for the way of escape. It will be there. God has promised to provide it. Take it.

For the Love of Money . . .

Read
1 TIMOTHY 6:3-10

The greatest blessings can turn into the greatest temptations.

Your World The 22-year-old, seven-foot pro-basketball star stood in front of several TV cameras after purchasing a 1.7-million-dollar Cape Cod-style house in central Florida. When asked to comment on the palatial beauty of his newly purchased home, the young athlete grinned, nodded his head, and began to sing a line from the Beatles' song "Money": "Just give me money, that's what I want!"

God's Word There is nothing wrong, of course, with making a lot of money. But the apostle Paul warned that the temptation to love money inordinately is especially strong and dangerous:

> People who want to get rich fall into temptation and a trap and into many foolish and harmful desires that plunge men into ruin and destruction. For the love of money is a root of all kinds of evil. Some people, eager for money, have wandered from the faith and pierced themselves with many griefs (1 Timothy 6:9-10).

Your Walk The young basketball star in the above scenario is traveling a dangerous road. But you don't have to be a young millionaire to fall into the temptation of inordinately loving money.

Review your check register. If most of your income goes to buy things of little eternal value, it's time to ask whether you love money too much. Use your money in the service of God and other people, and God will bless you with the material goods you need.

The Devil's End

Read
REVELATION 20:7-10

God assures us that the devil will get his due.

As we saw earlier, the devil has been in the temptation business for a long time—from the first days of human history. And we have to admit, he's performed his vile craft remarkably well. That's bad news for us, the objects of his assaults.

But the devil's days are numbered, and he knows it. His eternal destiny is fixed, and it isn't pretty. In the Book of Revelation, the apostle John reveals that Satan and his helpers will get the eternal reward they deserve:

> The devil, who deceived [God's people], was thrown into the lake of burning sulfur, where the beast and the false prophet had been thrown. They will be tormented day and night for ever and ever (Revelation 20:10).

The result? A beautiful one. As a resident of the new heaven and new earth, you will never again experience temptation. Neither Satan, nor his demons, nor the people he has used in your life to tempt you will be anywhere near you. They will be in the lake of fire. You'll never be tempted again.

That's good news. Remember it when you feel discouraged over your sin. When you feel as though you'll never improve your relationship with your spouse. When you despair about losing weight. When you cry over your lust. When you lose your temper yet again.

Look forward to an eternity of no temptation. And give thanks to God that He gives you such a promise to encourage you in time.

Hidden Addictions

The subject of addictions usually
conjures up visions of heroin shooters,
dope smokers, or cocaine snorters
huddled in dark, dirty alleyways engaged
in illegal activities. But decent, law-abiding
Christians can be addicted to behaviors and
substances that may be legal, but still harmful.
These people just hide behind a mask,
pretending to be what they're not.

In your quiet times this week,
let the Holy Spirit reveal to your heart
any *hidden addiction* you may be battling.
He will heal you, but you must first
remove the mask.

Unmasking Hidden Addictions

Read
ISAIAH 44:6-23

Anything that stands between you and God will cause you to fall.

Your World   The term *addiction* is often used today to describe anything from habitual drug abuse to the hobby of collecting baseball trading cards. The Latin root is *addicene,* which means "to give assent, to assign, or surrender." In ancient times the word was used to describe someone who was captured and kept in bondage.

All addictions have this in common:

- They remove us from our true feelings and provide a form of escape.
- They totally control the addict, and the control transcends logic.
- They always involve pleasure.
- They are ultimately destructive.
- They take top priority over all other life issues.
- They involve psychological dependence.
- Addicts deny their addiction.

God's Word   What is an addiction from God's perspective? If it has top priority in your life, it is an idol—a false god that you turn to for help and relief. "From the rest he makes a god, his idol; he bows down to it and worships. He prays to it and says, 'Save me; you are my god'" (Isaiah 44:17).

Your Walk   In this section of readings we are going to examine some common hidden addictions and expose the truth about each one with the light of God's Word. Be honest with yourself, and ask God to open your eyes to any existing or potential addiction in your life.

Codependency: Addiction to Rescuing

Read
PHILIPPIANS 3:10-21

Codependent people are often the barrier between God and a person who needs Him.

Your World Codependency is "sick love." It is something good taken to an unhealthy extreme. People who are addicted to helping, or "rescuers," often have low self-esteem, and they associate their self-worth with their ability to solve other people's problems. Codependency becomes an addiction when used as an escape from a person's own problems or insecurities, or sometimes masochism and self-denial give the codependent person a perverse sense of pleasure.

God's Word Obviously, God is not against us loving or helping others in need. Sometimes sacrificial love is necessary. (If not, Christ's sacrifice would mean nothing!)

The problem arises when your care for another person does nothing but enable him or her to continue in sin. Also, your life gradually centers on a troubled person, instead of on God. "No one can serve two masters. Either he will hate the one and love the other, or he will be devoted to the one and despise the other" (Matthew 6:24).

Your Walk If you are codependent, you ultimately could be causing the focus of your love more harm than good. Healthy love is the result of loving God first and foremost. Only then are we free to set appropriate boundaries in our relationships and not . cling. And that releases dependent people to face their own problems and rely on God for their solutions.

The Church and Sexaholism

Read
1 CORINTHIANS 6:18-20

Next to His Son, your sexuality is one of God's greatest gifts to you. Cherish it.

Your World   Can a man or woman really become a "sexaholic"? Dr. Archibald Hart believes so for several reasons. Sex provides pleasure, both physiological and psychological. Sex also generates a cycle of creating and reducing tension, and it stimulates excitement.

Sexual addictions generally fall into three categories: lustful addictions (excessive sexual desire—more likely in men), addictions to love and relationships (more likely in women), and perversions (distorted sexual practices).

God's Word   Sexual addictions distort one's perception of sex and the opposite sex (sometimes even the same sex). Sexual abuse or misinformation, fueled by guilt, is often at the root of sexual addiction.

This is why God set restrictions on our sexuality—not to limit our pleasure, but to enhance it. In fact, the complementing physical differences between men and women attest to God's desire for us to enjoy one another. "Male and female he created them. God blessed them and said to them, 'Be fruitful and increase in number' " (Genesis 1:27-28).

Your Walk   Do you struggle with sexual addiction? Repent and ask God for His insight, strength, and protection. But don't allow Satan to twist your repentance into guilt-absorbed self-hatred. That will only exacerbate the problem. God wants you to celebrate the sexuality He created for your pleasure.

Committed Believer or Religious Addict?

Read
MATTHEW 22:37

Even Christian trappings can trap us in the sin of idolatry.

Your World   Nathan is a new believer who can't think or talk about anything else but Jesus Christ. He's consumed with his new faith and wants to know everything about it. Whenever he is alone, he prays, reads his Bible, or listens to Bible-teaching tapes.

Then there's Chuck, who takes his Bible everywhere—even when he walks his dog! He never reads it, but he panics at the thought of not having his Bible with him at all times. He just feels safe with it at his side.

God's Word   Who's the addict and who's the on-fire believer?

> Although they claimed to be wise, they became fools and exchanged the glory of the immortal God for images. . . . They exchanged the truth of God for a lie, and worshiped and served created things rather than the Creator—who is forever praised. Amen (Romans 1:22-23,25).

Your Walk   Nathan is like most new Christians (and a few older saints). He is seeking to strengthen his faith in the true Christ through prayer and the study of God's Word.

On the other hand, Chuck is a "Bible-holic"; he has made the Bible an object of devotion instead of a tool used to grow in a deeper relationship with Christ. He sees it as a shortcut to the "peace that passes all understanding."

In what is your faith and devotion placed? A religious object or practice? Or a living Lord and Savior?

Polite Society's Pet Narcotic: Caffeine

Read
1 CORINTHIANS
10:23-33

Whether one snorts, injects, or sips from a demitasse cup, addiction is addiction.

Your World Right up there with alcohol and nicotine, caffeine is common in the world of mind-altering drugs abused by "nice people." Caffeine is a chemical found in coffee, tea, cocoa, chocolate, and many soft drinks, prescriptions, and over-the-counter drugs.

In large quantities, caffeine has acute and chronic effects on behavior, emotions, and body systems. For instance, it

- stimulates the central nervous system,
- increases activity levels, reduces fatigue, and heightens alertness,
- creates a state of high tension,
- increases the risk of panic attacks.

God's Word If the above side effects are true (especially the last two), should a Christian consume excessive amounts of caffeine or become dependent upon it? Not if the caffeine in any way hinders one's ability to worship and serve God. "Whether you eat or drink or whatever you do, do it all for the glory of God" (1 Corinthians 10:31).

Your Walk If you are addicted to caffeine, your first step to healing is to realize that excessive caffeine is harmful to your health. Then begin to gradually reduce your caffeine intake. You may want to begin exchanging your coffee or cola with fruit juice, herbal tea, or water. Like the previous addictions we have studied, caffeine only becomes a problem when your faith is placed in it instead of in God.

12 Steps to Freedom

Read
PHILIPPIANS 2:13

Christ can free you from any addiction.

Some former alcoholics developed the 12 steps now used by Alcoholics Anonymous. The Institute for Christian Living has revised them with a biblical perspective. They can help conquer any addition.

1. Admit your need for salvation.
2. Believe that a Power who came in the person of Christ can transform your weaknesses into strengths.
3. Turn your will and your life over to the care of Jesus Christ.
4. Take a fearless inventory of yourself—strengths and weaknesses.
5. Admit to Christ, yourself, and someone else the exact nature of your sins.
6. Be ready to have Christ heal all of these defects of character.
7. Ask Christ to transform all shortcomings.
8. List everyone you have harmed and become willing to make amends.
9. Make direct amends to such persons whenever possible.
10. Continue to take personal inventory and promptly admit when you are wrong.
11. Seek through prayer and meditation to improve your relationship with Jesus Christ.
12. Willingly share the message of Christ's love and forgiveness with others and practice these principles for spiritual living in all your affairs.

Whatever your addiction is, give it to God today. "For God is at work within you, helping you want to obey him, and then helping you do what he wants" (Philippians 2:13 TLB).

*Whoever
dies with
the most toys . . .
dies with
nothing.*

Materialism

The advertising industry wants to convince Americans that they can and must have it all— right now. And this strategy is working.

Consumer debt is skyrocketing, while consumer saving drops every year. Americans are financing their quest for fulfillment through the material rather than the spiritual. But by God's design, we can only be satisfied by the spiritual—the indwelling of the Holy Spirit.

During your quiet times this week, honestly evaluate any materialistic tendencies you may have as you read about some victims of and victors over *materialism*.

Materialism Leaves Us Empty-Handed

Read
EPHESIANS 5

The wealth of the world pales in comparison to the riches of God.

Your World   Among the wealthy and elite residents of New York City, there is a man who collects rare and valuable jewelry, silverware, and furniture. One day several years ago he bought some large canvases, cheap paint, and a roller. He indiscriminately rolled different colors of paint onto the canvases and placed them on his walls. On the corner of each canvas he attached a price tag that read: "$200,000." As he expected, when the burglars came, they took the worthless paintings, leaving behind the priceless treasures.

God's Word   That's exactly what happens to us when we fall into the trap of materialism. "For of this you can be sure: No immoral, impure or greedy person—such a man is an idolater—has any inheritance in the kingdom of Christ and of God" (Ephesians 5:5). What may seem valuable from the world's perspective may actually cost us that which is truly priceless: our souls.

Your Walk   When you devote yourself to the acquisition of big houses, designer clothes, expensive cars, and exotic vacations, you sink to the level of the New York City burglars. And you cheat yourself out of the eternal riches God has set aside for those who devote their lives to Him.

This week as we look at the plague of materialism, ask God to show you the things you have placed in front of Him. Then remove them.

Mansions on Earth and in Heaven

Read
LUKE 12:13-21

No mansion on earth can stand next to the mansion that waits for you in heaven.

Your World   Wes and Lisa Campbell are both in their mid-thirties and have a combined income of 100,000 dollars. During their ten-year marriage, their dream has been to own a house in prestigious Oxford Estates where the average cost of a house is 300,000 dollars.

They worked hard, even on Sundays. They put off having children. They sacrificed. And three months ago they moved into their dream: a 6,000-square-foot, 12-room, 325,000-dollar house on a three-acre lot.

Wes and Lisa finally had an address that mattered. Unfortunately, they had only enough furniture for four rooms. They didn't anticipate their utility bill quadrupling. The expenses for weekly lawn care, not to mention the upkeep, are endless. And the taxes!

After two months, the burden became too great. They put their dream house up for sale.

God's Word   Wes and Lisa learned the hard way that sacrificing for worldly achievements and belongings is futile. "Their destiny is destruction, their god is their stomach, and their glory is in their shame. Their mind is on earthly things. But our citizenship is in heaven" (Philippians 3:19-20).

Your Walk   Owning a home in a prominent area of town is not bad in and of itself. Only when your devotion to it surpasses your devotion to God does it become a threat to your relationship with God.

101

Sometimes It's the Little Things

Read
2 CORINTHIANS 4:16-18

Principles based on eternal values enable us to endure any trial.

Your World Rob and Helen Fisher have a simple, frugal life-style. They have four children, ages 3-11, who keep them both very busy.

It's sometimes difficult for Rob and Helen because they don't have extra money to buy as many extras as the kids' friends seem to get.

Rob makes enough to support the family. They could make more, however. But Rob and Helen made the decision years ago that Helen would stay home and raise the children. They know the investment of themselves into the lives of their children is far more valuable than the sacrifice necessary for material gain.

God's Word It doesn't have to be a big house or an expensive car. Materialism sometimes comes disguised as the little extras. "For our light and momentary troubles are achieving for us an eternal glory that far outweighs them all" (2 Corinthians 4:17).

Your Walk As Christians, we must be able to discern between "needs" and "wants." When we have the discipline to say no to things that are of no eternal value, we are saying no to materialism.

Don't let materialism blind you to the people in your life who need you. It may be your spouse, children, or parents. Trust God to provide for your needs. He will reward you in heaven for choosing that which is of eternal value over that which is eternally worthless.

Feeding the Hungry Instead of the Full

Read
LUKE 16:19-31

Materialism blinds us to the needs of others.

Your World Stan Waters is a partner at one of Chicago's top CPA firms. Once a year, the firm hosts a sumptuous seven-course steak-and-lobster dinner for its clients and employees in an exclusive club downtown. Every year Stan stays home.

The reason? Stan grieves that thousands of dollars are being spent on a catered meal to feed already-well-fed people when the city is teeming with those who are hungry and homeless. He has instructed the firm to calculate the cost of his and his wife's meals and donate the amount to the nearest homeless shelter.

God's Word Stan's sacrifice won't feed and shelter all the hungry and homeless in Chicago, but it will take care of about 25 "Lazaruses" at the shelter.

> There was a rich man who was dressed in purple and fine linen and lived in luxury every day. At his gate was laid a beggar named Lazarus, covered with sores and longing to eat what fell from the rich man's table (Luke 16:19-21).

Your Walk The cold, harsh weather of winter is the most dreaded time of year for homeless people. Take a good look at the food and clothing you have and determine what your family can sacrifice for those less fortunate. Make it a family activity. It may become a project you'll repeat every year.

People Have More Value Than Things

Read
MATTHEW 6:19-24

Children learn the value of other people only when they realize their own infinite worth.

Your World Seven-year-old Amy Packard's favorite thing in the world was a crystal pitcher her mother had received as a wedding gift. It was engraved with her mother's monogram in Gothic lettering. Amy thought it was exquisite.

One day Amy was in her playhouse preparing for a make-believe tea party. She decided the crystal pitcher would be the perfect touch. She sneaked it out of the china cabinet, slinked through the back door, stumbled, and dropped the pitcher on the patio pavement.

In tearful hysterics, Amy sat surrounded by broken glass. She had destroyed the most beautiful thing in the world.

Amy's mother carried her inside and tried to calm her. She kept asking Amy if she was hurt, but all Amy could think about was the pitcher (and a spanking).

Her mother said, "Don't worry, Amy. It's only a thing. You're much more valuable than any thing—even that pitcher."

God's Word By God's grace, Amy had a mother who understood the value of a person over a thing.

> Do not store up for yourselves treasures on earth, where moth and rust destroy, and where thieves break in and steal. . . . For where your treasure is, there your heart will be also (Matthew 6:19,21).

Your Walk Children learn some of life's most valuable lessons by observing their parents' behavior. Discourage materialism in your children's lives by loving them more than things.

Materialism

Read
LUKE 18:18-25

*A life spent
pursuing
material goods
is an eternity
wasted.*

The old adage still rings true: "You can't take it with you." No matter the extent of your material wealth, you will eventually lose it all. The choice is yours. You can release it now into God's service, or you can wait until death snatches it from your grasp.

Remember the conversation between Jesus and the rich ruler, a willing victim of materialism:

> A certain ruler asked him, "Good teacher, what must I do to inherit eternal life? . . . Jesus answered . . . "You know the commandments. . . ." "All these I have kept since I was a boy," he said. When Jesus heard this, he said to him, "You still lack one thing. Sell everything you have and give to the poor, and you will have treasure in heaven. Then come, follow me." When he heard this, he became very sad, because he was a man of great wealth. Jesus looked at him and said, "How hard it is for the rich to enter the kingdom of God!" (Luke 18:18-24).

What "one thing" did the rich ruler lack? Faith, along with the knowledge that he was going to lose it all anyway. He foolishly opted for earthly wealth instead of heavenly treasures.

Does Jesus ask everyone to sell everything? No. But Jesus knew the rich man's heart: His faith was in his wealth. And in the end, his materialism would be his eternal destruction. That is the heinous lie of materialism. We think it's all ours, but it never was.

Loneliness

In the midst of holiday fun and festivities, *loneliness* is usually not an issue we care to think about too much. However, Christians need to be aware that special holidays like Thanksgiving and Christmas can be lonely times for the single, divorced, widowed, poor, or homeless. And even though God's Word comforts us with the knowledge that none of us is ever really alone (Psalm 139), people still need people.

As you study loneliness during your quiet times this week, ask God to make you more sensitive to those who need your friendship. And if you are currently experiencing loneliness, ask your best Friend to use this time to draw you closer to Himself.

You'll Never Walk Alone

Read
PSALM 139:7-10

The Lord is an inseparable companion, always and everywhere.

Your World "I'm running away!" declares the angry five-year-old. Teddy bear in hand, he slams the kitchen door, trudges through the front yard, and sets out for the world.

He doesn't see the concerned but loving eyes watching through the kitchen window, nor does he hear the quiet footsteps that soon follow him. His mother plays along, but stays close enough to provide protection should he stray too far.

God's Word As the ultimate loving Parent, God allows each of us to set our own course. But we never get out of His sight.

David, the psalmist, realized that he could go nowhere that would be out of the LORD's presence. He would never be truly alone:

> Where can I go from your Spirit? Where can I flee from your presence? If I go up to the heavens, you are there; if I make my bed in the depths, you are there. If I rise on the wings of the dawn, if I settle on the far side of the sea, even there your hand will guide me, your right hand will hold me fast (Psalm 139:7-10).

Your Walk This week as you think about loneliness, friends and relatives will come to mind who long for a "travel partner." You'll also reflect on those times when you, too, feel alone. Fix your mind on the fact that there's never a place and never a time that lacks the presence of God.

The Hardest Friend to Make

Read
PSALM 8:3-5

We can love ourselves because we know God loves us.

Your World "Why do I have so much trouble making friends?" The young woman's words were as much an outcry of frustration as a question.

The pastor, who knew her well, had a quiet but surprising answer. "You'll never have a good friend until you make one specific friend: yourself."

For many of us, it's easier to love almost anyone than to love ourselves. We know all too well our own shortcomings.

God's Word For good reason, Jesus tells us to "love your neighbor as yourself." Knowing my value in God's eyes must come first, and it's built on a strong foundation: God, who created us, loves us. He considers us the crown of creation.

> When I consider your heavens, the work of your fingers, the moon and the stars, which you have set in place, what is man that you are mindful of him, the son of man that you care for him? You made him a little lower than the heavenly beings and crowned him with glory and honor (Psalm 8:3-5).

And to God, we were, as the saying goes, to die for.

Your Walk Don't be deluded by negative thoughts about yourself. God's Word gives reason for a positive self-acceptance. We're created in His own image, and He loves us more deeply than we can ever love ourselves.

Much of the ache of loneliness is cast out when we build that most difficult of all friendships: friendship with ourselves.

109

Only
the Lonely

Read
PSALM 68:5-6

*The lonely
and troubled
have a
special place
in the heart
of God.*

Your World During the Vietnam War, American prisoners were often kept in isolation as a means of pressure. Many captives were psychologically devastated by the days and nights of total silence.

But one prisoner, who later wrote a book titled *In the Presence of Mine Enemies,* found that God's presence became more real to him as he clung to memorized Scripture and prayer. When all other hope was gone, the Lord was faithful.

God's Word Throughout Scripture, God is revealed to us as having a special concern for the outcast, the lonely, the poor, the disenfranchised. His Son, Jesus, consistently sought out those whom society had abandoned.

Once again, the psalmist brings us special hope for the lonely: "A father to the fatherless, a defender of widows, is God in his holy dwelling. God sets the lonely in families, he leads forth the prisoners with singing; but the rebellious live in a sunscorched land" (Psalm 68:5-6).

Your Walk Not only can we be assured that God has a special concern for the lonely, but He calls us to act on that concern. As the Spirit leads, list the names of hurting people who need to know the Lord's special concern for them. Then pray for their individual needs, asking God to reveal to you how you can share the love of Christ with them today.

Come Together

Read
HEBREWS 10:24-25

Christian fellowship casts out loneliness.

Your World   Have you ever been lonely in a crowded room? Have you ever traveled alone to a large city where you knew no one?

It's not the quantity of people that makes for good fellowship, but the quality of the relationships. The busier we become these days, the more often we feel the loss of true community. We need a place where, as the old "Cheers" theme said, "Everybody knows your name." But the friendships depicted on television are usually the stuff of fantasy.

God's Word   The Bible describes one true home for intimate fellowship: the church. When we come together as the people of faith, something exciting happens: We become the body of Christ.

But times were hectic in the first century, too, and the author of Hebrews issued a word of caution:

> And let us consider how we may spur one another on toward love and good deeds. Let us not give up meeting together, as some are in the habit of doing, but let us encourage one another—and all the more as you see the Day approaching (Hebrews 10:24-25).

Your Walk   The church should be more than a social club. Special relationships should be developed there. We grow through encouragement from God's family, and when we reach out to encourage others.

How's your church life? Ask God to show you how to offer your gifts to the body of Christ.

The Art of Content-ment

Read
PHILIPPIANS 4:11-13

We can't always control our circumstances, but God gives us peace in the midst of them.

Your World Day after day, his eyesight failing, the prisoner sat in his damp cell as his hour of execution approached. There were so many places he needed to be, so much still to be done. How could God desire that his life fade out this way?

Yet, in these very circumstances, Paul wrote one of the most positive, vibrant letters in literary history. His letter to the Philippians shines with hope and joy.

God's Word Paul understood that God was in control, that He would work out His purpose. And while he longed for the comfort of friends like Timothy, deeper than his loneliness was a joy in the Christ who knew what was best for him and orchestrated the circumstances of his life.

> For I have learned to be content whatever the circumstances. I know what it is to be in need, and I know what it is to have plenty. I have learned the secret of being content in any and every situation, whether well fed or hungry, whether living in plenty or in want. I can do everything through him who gives me strength (Philippians 4:11-13).

Your Walk What does it take for you to be happy? Do you need the right friends around you, the right things? Or does your contentment rest with the only Source to whom you can trust it?

As you pray today, ask God to help you cultivate the art of being "content whatever the circumstances."

Loneliness

Read
MARK 14:35-36

Lonely times can be lovely times when we grow closer to the Lord.

One of the first recorded statements of our Lord is: "It is not good for the man to be alone" (Genesis 2:18). We agree, and we try to plan our lives to keep loneliness out. But can loneliness be a good thing? Is it always to be avoided?

Jesus faced that question 2000 years ago. He used a solitary time in the desert to grow stronger in His calling. There Satan tempted Him unsuccessfully with the lure of popularity.

And while He was constantly surrounded by crowds, even His closest disciples frequently misunderstood Him.

Perhaps His loneliest hour came in the Garden of Gethsemane:

> Going a little farther, he fell to the ground and prayed that if possible the hour might pass from him. "Abba, Father," he said, "everything is possible for you. Take this cup from me. Yet not what I will, but what you will" (Mark 14:35-36).

The loneliness was intense, painful. But Jesus knew it was necessary. It prepared Him for the final road He had to travel alone . . . to a cross.

Life brings us crises that must be faced alone but that draw us closest to God. As in the story of Job, friends' voices can drown out His voice. Loneliness can bring a new depth to our love for the Lord—a depth that might not have been otherwise possible.

Yet when we face those trials, we know that He has been down that road before us. We also know that He goes with us.

113

*Rich indeed
is the one
who is content
with the
simple things
of life.*

Contentment

We sometimes find ourselves in situations that are stressful, heartbreaking, even dangerous. The trauma in your life may be sickness, financial ruin, or a destroyed relationship.

For the apostle Paul (and for some believers today) it was persecution for his faith. Christians were and are being executed for simply being Christians.

During your quiet times this week, you will be encouraged by the words of the apostle Paul and others who discovered *contentment* in the midst of life's severest trials.

Contentment Is No Fairy Tale

Read
JOHN 10:10

We find contentment not by gaining anything but by losing everything.

Your World   "Are you content now?" the caterpillar asked Alice in Wonderland. "Well, I should like to be a little larger," she said. "Three inches is such a wretched height to be. . . . I'm not used to it!"

It's curious how most of us are like Alice: We concentrate on that which seems "wretched" about our circumstances. "I don't deserve this!" we tell ourselves. We want things to change. We want to be "larger."

Unfortunately, we are unlike Alice in that the challenges of our lives are not dreams. They are reality. And a person who is content, no matter what, is a person God can use.

God's Word   Webster defines *contented* as "manifesting satisfaction with one's posses- sions, status, or situation." The apostle Paul would have concurred with Webster, but would have submitted a more complete defi- nition—one referring to the Source of con- tentment:

> I have learned to be content whatever the circumstances. I know what it is to be in need, and I know what it is to have plenty. I have learned the secret of being content in any and every situa- tion. . . . I can do everything through him who gives me strength (Philippians 4:11-13).

Your Walk   Have you learned that nothing in this world satisfies? This week discover the key to contentment that God has provided to all who faithfully seek it.

The Poisonous Presence of Pride

Read
PROVERBS 11:2

Contentment results when we get off the throne and bow before the rightful Ruler.

Your World Church tradition tells us pride is the first deadly sin or, as popularly phrased, "the mother of all sins." And no sin destroys contentment in our lives more than pride.

Pride prevails in our culture. We have ejected God from the throne of our lives and installed ourselves in His place. We want control. We want to be accountable to no one. And when we fail, we try to find someone else to blame.

God's Word "Blessed are the poor in spirit, for theirs is the kingdom of heaven" (Matthew 5:3). To be "poor in spirit" is simply to be without pride. It is not only to know that you do not have control, but also to regret ever trying to take control. In fact, there remains no desire for control.

Your Walk Not all pride is bad. The pride or satisfaction you feel when you admire the work of your hands or mind is not sinful pride. In fact, "God saw all that he had made, and it was very good" (Genesis 1:31).

The pride condemned in Scripture is the self-centeredness at the heart of sin. It is what compelled Eve to eat the forbidden fruit. She wanted to seize the throne of control from God for herself.

Is pride keeping you from the contentment God has for you? Examine your heart, and ask God to show you who is on the throne of your heart. If *you* are, then move.

117

Content in the Midst of Grief

Read
1 PETER 1:3-12

Those who suffer the most are those whose contentment shines the brightest.

Your World The elderly couple stands in front of the smoldering, charred remains of their home—the one they built 53 years ago as newlyweds. Everything Gene and Ruth own has been reduced to ashes. But in the midst of the shock, they cling to each other. Tears of joy trace around their smiles.

Television reporters ask questions about grief and loss. The man and woman respond with words of hope and praise to God. "We're still in God's hands. I just thank Him for protecting my Ruthie," Gene says softly. He then motions to the remains. "All of this is nothing." And the community watches, incredulous and awestruck.

God's Word Contentment in the wake of a tragedy? It's a contradiction in the world's eyes. But the believer sees the presence of God and the power of His love to bring peace and contentment in any situation, especially in times of sorrow.

> In this you greatly rejoice, though now for a little while you may have had to suffer grief in all kinds of trials (1 Peter 1:6).

Your Walk What does the world see when you "suffer grief in all kinds of trials"? Contentment fueled by faith? Or moaning fueled by self-pity?

If you are grieving over a situation, ask God to pour out His grace on your life. He will give you the kind of contentment that perplexes the world.

Sharing in God's Mercy

Read
1 TIMOTHY 1:15-16

Mercy can evict our pain and invite contentment to reside permanently.

Your World Jacinta Diaz was known as a great woman of faith in her church in Puerto Rico. People usually turned to Jacinta for prayer in times of trouble. One night her son got into a nasty argument. Minutes later he was dead.

Words of the tragedy reached Jacinta's neighborhood. Friends rushed to her side and grieved with her. In the meantime, the assailant was overcome with remorse. He couldn't believe what he had done. He begged someone to get Jacinta to pray for him. He didn't know he had killed her son.

When Jacinta heard of his request, she walked a half mile to meet him. There she laid her hands on her son's killer and prayed with him.

God's Word Mercy. It's a mark of a child of God. And if mercy is absent from a life, contentment may be as well.

If we freely receive God's mercy, we need to freely give it—even to those who hurt us. Remember the words of Jesus: "Father, forgive them, for they do not know what they are doing" (Luke 23:34).

Your Walk Think about the last time someone hurt you. Did you vow revenge? Cry out in anger? Build a protective wall around your heart?

Remember Jacinta's prayer for her son's killer, and Jesus' prayer for those who demanded His crucifixion. Contentment is found not in withholding mercy but in freely giving it.

119

Having the Heart of Jesus Christ

Read
1 TIMOTHY 6:3-11

Pure hearts have a clear and distinct purpose: to serve and please God.

Your World In the Beatitudes, Jesus says, "Blessed are the pure in heart, for they will see God" (Matthew 5:8). But how can sinners be pure in heart?

The Greek word for *pure* in this case means unmixed, unadulterated. So Jesus is referring to a singularity of purpose. Those who are pure in heart are not double-minded or unstable in their walk with God; they do not waffle on their convictions (see James 1:6-8). And when a heart beats only for God, Jesus promises contentment.

God's Word But is it possible to have a pure heart in a sinful world and, at the same time, be content? According to the apostle Paul, that is just what every Christian should strive to achieve. It's part of the Good News.

> But godliness with contentment is great gain. . . . But you, man of God . . . pursue righteousness, godliness, faith, love, endurance and gentleness (1 Timothy 6:6,11).

Your Walk If having a pure heart seems impossible, keep in mind that all you need to do or be has been accomplished through Jesus Christ. Only in Christ can you be content in the assurance that, by God's grace, the life of His perfect Son has become your life. When God sees you, He sees Jesus.

When your heart is pure, contentment is the natural consequence. Ask God to renew in you the heart of Jesus.

Contentment

Read
PHILIPPIANS 4:4-7

Being content begins with knowing that God is all we will ever need.

A mother who wanted to encourage her son's musical talent took him to a performance by Ignace Paderewski, Poland's famous pianist and prime minister. They took their seats at the front of the auditorium. The mother soon began conversing with a friend and, without her noticing, the little boy slipped away.

At 8 P.M. the house lights dimmed, the crowd quieted, and the curtain opened. The mother, to her horror, saw not Ignace Paderewski seated at the grand Steinway, but her son—plunking out "Twinkle, Twinkle, Little Star."

Paderewski appeared and moved quickly to the keyboard. "Don't quit—keep playing," he whispered to the boy. Leaning over the boy, the master filled in a bass part with his left hand and added a running obbligato with his right. The crowd sat mesmerized.

Our study on contentment boils down to one truth: When we receive Christ as our Savior, a new life begins in us. We are new creatures (2 Corinthians 5:17). And with that new life comes power—the Master's power to transform our discordant attempts at righteousness into a beautiful symphony of praise to God. We then are content with who and what we are because of who He is.

It was with this knowledge that the writer of Hebrews could say: "Be content with what you have, because God has said, 'Never will I leave you' " (Hebrews 13:5).

*The key
to a great
relationship:
Be a
good friend.*

Relationships

Relationships can bring us the greatest joys.
And the deepest sorrows. Misunderstandings.
Selfish motives. Dishonesty. Such things rip
apart bonds that were once close and strong.

But you can take steps to make sure that never
happens. This week during your search of the
Scriptures, discover five steps to relating to
other people God's way. Because when you do,
your relationships will seem like a little bit of
heaven on earth.

Soft Words for a Hard World

Read
MATTHEW 9:35-38

Relationships thrive when compassion is the driving force behind them.

Your World Hard-heartedness? Cold-heartedness? There's plenty of that in our world. But tenderheartedness . . . what's that?

It's the mom who holds the hurting child on her lap. It's the dad who listens quietly to his son's fears, offering comfort and encouragement. It's the friend who sees you dragging behind, runs back, puts his arm around you, and says, "Come on, I'll walk with you."

God's Word Colossians 3:12 calls it "compassion": "Therefore, as God's chosen people, holy and dearly loved, clothe yourselves with compassion." Compassion is the ability to "feel for" someone who hurts. To put yourself in his or her place. To listen with sympathy and to offer words of comfort.

It's easy to be harsh, to put down, to lash out, even to kick people when they're down. But Paul says, in effect, "Do you want a good relationship? Then be tenderhearted toward others."

Your Walk "Be hard on yourself; be tender to others." Perhaps that tender mercy is what we're striving for. Sure, we should be firm. But sometimes what is really needed is a soft cushion of compassion that people can lean on and know they won't be driven away.

A compassionate person is hard to find. Just the same, if someone needs one today, let it be you.

124

Try a Little Kindness

Read
JOHN 5:1-15

Kindness reaches out in love to others, building strong relationships.

Your World Someone once said, "Be kind; everyone you meet is fighting a battle." How true. We often think we're the only ones struggling. But in this sin-shackled world of ours, everyone is fighting a tough battle of some kind.

How can you make another person's way a little easier? With kindness.

God's Word The apostle Paul addressed kindness with the believers in Ephesus: "Get rid of all bitterness, rage and anger, brawling and slander, along with every form of malice. Be kind and compassionate to one another, forgiving each other, just as in Christ God forgave you" (Ephesians 4:31-32).

The word *kind* means "mild, pleasant, gracious, benevolent." When a kind person sees a need, he offers help. When a kind person has been wronged, he reacts mildly.

Your Walk In a world brimming with coldness, it's not easy to find kindness. But Christians are to be characterized by it. God desires that we go out of our way to meet a need, offer a hand, love a hurting soul.

Kindness starts with our thoughts, seasons our words, and works its way through our actions. Think kindly and you will speak kindly and act kindly.

What are your thoughts today? Are you angry, upset, even seething inside? Or can you set your mind on the things above so that you can do something kind here below?

The Doorway of Humility

Read
JOHN 13:1-17

Christians are not to be doormats but doorways for others to enter Christ's rest.

Your World "Humility is strange," the well-known adage goes. "The moment you think you've got it, you've lost it." Humility is the opposite of self-centeredness. A humble person listens, cares, gives. He thinks not of himself, but of others—their needs, their feelings.

God's Word Jesus personified humility. Consider His words in Matthew 11:28-30: "Come to me, all you who are weary and burdened, and I will give you rest. Take my yoke upon you and learn from me, for I am gentle and humble in heart, and you will find rest for your souls. For my yoke is easy and my burden is light."

The word *humility* means to "assign yourself a lower rank or place," to "put yourself below" others. That's tough. But we have a Savior who's been there to help us live it out.

Your Walk Does humility mean we should be a "doormat"? No. But it does mean we go out of our way to love other people, no matter what they intend to do to us.

Jesus' example is astonishing. He was God incarnate, yet when His disciples balked at serving, He doffed His robes and washed their feet. Then He told them, "Do as I have done to you."

That goes for us, too. And He's ready to give us the strength we need to obey Him.

How to Inherit the Earth

Read
MATTHEW 19:13-14

Meekness is exemplified by Jesus Christ and expressed in healthy relationships.

Your World Meekness is not a popular attribute. People think of a meek person as the mousy guy who never speaks up, who lets people walk all over him, who smiles weakly even though he may be steaming inside.

But meekness is not weakness; it's power under control. It's pictured by a powerful horse obediently responding to the slightest pull of the reins.

God's Word True meekness is essential in all our relationships. Jesus said, "Blessed are the meek, for they will inherit the earth" (Matthew 5:5).

Why is that true? Because the meek are not hard, rough, overbearing. They express themselves gently, but firmly. They know how to work through relationships and help other people succeed.

Jesus was meek and gentle (see Matthew 11:28-30). It's that very meekness that makes us feel joy and comfort in His presence.

Your Walk Meekness is the mom with a million responsibilities who, with God's help, is able to maintain her cool with three cranky kids. It's the worker who willingly stays late to help the boss prepare for an important presentation.

We can become meek and gentle through the power of the Spirit and the free choice of our wills. It's not an easy choice, but it's a choice that will ignite our relationships.

It Takes Patience to Build Patience

Read
LUKE 22:31-34

Patience means never giving up— even when everyone else says you should.

Your World "Love is patient, love is kind." So wrote the apostle Paul in 1 Corinthians 13:4. Put your own name in place of the word *love* in that passage and see how it comes out:

- "John is patient . . ." for a while, until he can't stand it anymore and explodes!
- "Sue is patient . . ." until she lets you have it a week later with bitter accusations!

God's Word What is patience? It's the ability to remain cool even when everyone else is heating up, to take it from others for as long as it takes.

The apostle Peter also wrote about patience: "The Lord is not slow in keeping his promise, as some understand slowness. He is patient with you, not wanting anyone to perish, but everyone to come to repentance" (2 Peter 3:9).

God is patient. He sticks it out, keeps waiting, doesn't give up. Because He loves us.

Your Walk Sometimes patience seems impossible to get or keep. If you pray for it, you may find your life becoming more tense and miserable than ever. That's because the only way God can build patience is by bringing you through situations where you must be patient! But that process produces a patience that will endure anything. And that's worth the cost.

128

Relationships

Read
1 PETER 3:8-9

*Clothing
ourselves in
godly attributes
will strengthen
and enrich our
relationships.*

The slightest misunderstanding can crush some relationships. Yet others are like rock—seemingly indestructible.

What makes the difference? In a Christian relationship that lasts, you'll inevitably find certain attributes in effect:

> Therefore, as God's chosen people, holy and dearly loved, clothe yourselves with compassion, kindness, humility, gentleness and patience (Colossians 3:12).

That phrase "clothe yourselves" means to cover yourself, to be entirely immersed in something, even hide completely inside something. We are to clothe ourselves with compassion, kindness, humility, gentleness, patience—five keys to healthy, rewarding relationships. In the previous five readings we've caught a biblical glimpse of each of those attributes.

Imagine befriending someone whose life could be described by those virtues. You would receive tender mercy when you made mistakes. When you were hurting, you would receive kindness. You would have someone who always exhibits humility and would listen, care, and serve. He or she would be gentle, not pushy or demanding. This person would work patiently with you, even if you missed it 100 times.

The amazing truth is that, in Christ, you can be that person today. Just by putting those key attributes to work in your life. When you do, you'll find your relationships becoming delightfully rewarding.

Life's Skills

*Synchronize
your priorities
with God.*

Priorities

Each year around New Year's Day we begin to
assess our accomplishments and failures
during the past 12 months. Then we make
new resolutions guaranteeing that we'll
triumph over the failures next year. And by
the end of the first week in January,
we've broken most of our resolutions.

What's the problem? *Priorities.* God has
a certain set of priorities that He wants
us to adhere to because He knows they are
the foolproof plan for a life full of peace and
wisdom. But they take commitment,
discipline, and time.

Align your priorities with God's priorities
throughout your quiet times this week.

Spiritual Maturity Is a Lifelong Process

Read
HEBREWS 12:1-12

When you experience the true God, nothing else in the world can satisfy you.

Your World Most Christians believe they need to get their spiritual lives in order. They admit they don't spend enough time nurturing their relationship with God through Bible study and prayer. God is not a priority.

Kurt D. Bruner says in *Responsible Living in an Age of Excuses* that there are several reasons for this. First, misconceptions about God can stifle commitment. Seek out a believer who has a balanced, committed faith and share your doubts and struggles.

Second, after you've pinpointed the errors, search for the truth of God's character in His Word. The more you know, the more you will want to know.

Third, don't try to replace your relationship with God with religious ritual. Like a marital relationship, commitment to and communication with God are critical.

God's Word How can you tell if someone has made God a top priority? In the words of the psalmist: "As the deer pants for streams of water, so my soul pants for you, O God. My soul thirsts for God, for the living God. When can I go and meet with God?" (Psalm 42:1-2).

Your Walk The degree of satisfaction you derive from your spiritual life depends on your choices. You can choose to remain a victim of religious distortion and disillusionment. Or you can seek the truth, which is the foundation for a balanced relationship with your heavenly Father.

134

Priorities for Our Relationships

Read
GENESIS 2:20-24

*A true friend
loves you
as you are
but doesn't
let you
stay that way.*

Your World   Human beings were not created for solitude. We want intimacy. However, we can be lured into a dysfunctional or codependent relationship out of a desperate need for love or belonging.

This can be unhealthy, even harmful, according to Kurt Bruner: "Countless relationships have been crippled by the notion that real love means accepting irresponsible behavior. But a distinction must be made between love and acceptance."

God's Word   The Bible makes it clear that exhorting our friends and loved ones to lead godly and productive lives is the highest of love's callings. It's called "tough love."

> As iron sharpens iron, so one man sharpens another (Proverbs 27:17).

Your Walk   Perfect relationships are nonexistent. But for healthy relationships, Bruner offers these suggestions:

- Do not allow your need for acceptance to compromise your goal of healthy relationships.
- Learn to balance unconditional love for people with conditional acceptance of behavior.
- Commit yourself to doing what's best for the other person.

Accepting or ignoring irresponsible behavior is not unconditional love. When we make healthy relationships a priority, we hold those we love accountable for their actions and choices, even when it hurts.

We Are Sinners, Not Victims

Read
ROMANS 7:14-19

Shifting blame cannot excuse your sins. But the cross can.

Your World Whether it's due to "blame-shift" psychology or "no-fault" theology, people today refuse to accept responsibility for their behavior. The explosion of AIDS, crime, sexual immorality, suicide, teen pregnancy, and drug and alcohol addictions can almost always be traced to the "victim's" reckless pursuit of personal pleasure without regard for the consequences.

Kurt Bruner says in *Responsible Living,*

> It is not individual sinful acts that create a cycle of destruction in our lives. Rather, it is the refusal to acknowledge them as such. . . . Consequently, true victimization occurs. We become victims, not to outside factors but to our own presumptions.

God's Word The truth is, we are each born with a sin nature. But Jesus Christ died to free us from the bondage of that sin nature.

The Bible tells us what happens if we don't repent of a sin as soon as it rears its ugly head in our lives: "Each one is tempted when, by his own evil desire, he is dragged away and enticed. Then, after desire has conceived, it gives birth to sin; and sin, when it is full-grown, gives birth to death" (James 1:14-15).

Your Walk Evaluate your moral priorities. Do you ever put doing what is right over your own desires? Doing right takes a stubborn commitment to achieving the eternal reward instead of the momentary pleasure.

136

On-the-Job Ethics and Priorities

Read
PROVERBS 10:4-5

*Satisfaction
and self-respect
come when
you know
you've given
your best.*

Your World According to a recent study, what was once known as the Protestant work ethic is absent from the American workplace. Why? In most cases, employees simply fail to put forth effort. We've become complacent, even irresponsible. The bottom line: Professional excellence is no longer a priority for employees.

God's Word Sometime between traveling, preaching, and tent-making, the apostle Paul wrote:

> Slaves, obey your earthly masters in everything; and do it, not only when their eye is on you and to win their favor, but with sincerity of heart and reverence for the Lord. Whatever you do, work at it with all your heart. . . . It is the Lord Christ you are serving (Colossians 3:22-24).

Your Walk If you are complacent and unenthusiastic about your work, you need to develop certain habits and priorities, says Kurt Bruner.

- Hold yourself accountable for your attitudes. Rise above the negativism that infects your job or workplace.
- Work with a purpose. Remember that your best effort is an expression of worship to the Lord.
- Pursue specific goals. Stretch yourself to achieve and learn more.
- Seek to serve. Put the success of the company, your boss, and those below you over your own.
- Work hard, but keep your job in balance with the rest of your life.

Good Stewardship Is Common Sense

Read
PROVERBS
6:6-8; 13:22a

Your financial priorities will impact the world for good or for bad.

Your World Our nation's finances are in shambles. Not only does the federal government have an enormous debt, but ordinary Americans are in the same sinking boat. Consumer debt has skyrocketed, and consumer saving has plummeted during the past generation.

As Christians we must abide by the Bible's admonitions for good stewardship. If you are in a financial quagmire, there's hope. You don't need to be a CPA or an MBA to prioritize your finances. All it takes is common sense and a little self-control.

God's Word Our financial priorities are important to God. The Bible has more to say about money than faith or prayer.

> So do not worry, saying, "What shall we eat?" or "What shall we drink?" or "What shall we wear?" For the pagans run after all these things, and your heavenly Father knows that you need them. But seek first his kingdom and his righteousness, and all these things will be given to you as well (Matthew 6:31-33).

Your Walk Kurt Bruner says in *Responsible Living* that the best financial advice from all the experts can be summed up in three basic principles.

- Spend less than you earn. Except for buying a house, avoid all debt.

- Give some. For Christians, giving is a responsibility and a privilege.

- Save some. Set saving goals (for a car, a boat, or your child's braces); plan for emergencies and retirement.

Setting Priorities

Read
JOHN 16:17-33

Setting and keeping priorities will help set and keep you on the road to honoring God.

As we have examined some principles for setting priorities in various aspects of our lives, one fact has become painfully obvious: Life is complicated, and there are no simple solutions.

Some of us have spiritual scars from involvement in abusive or legalistic religions. Some of us are suffering in unhealthy relationships that drain our energy and suffocate our joy. Some of us have been in bondage to immorality for so long that there doesn't seem to be any hope. Some of us have blown it professionally and are praying for just one more chance. And some of us are drowning in debt that seems to grow exponentially.

But trouble never surprised Jesus. In John's Gospel, Jesus warned His disciples about their impending trials. And then He offered hope: "I have told you these things, so that in me you may have peace. In this world you will have trouble. But take heart! I have overcome the world" (John 16:33).

Setting and even keeping the biblical priorities we discussed this week will not solve your problems overnight. But they are the best place to start. They are a paradigm for a life that is balanced and functional.

In the meantime, your top priority as a Christian should be to maintain your commitment to living a life full of peace, a life that glorifies God and testifies to the world of His love and power.

*Work done
for the Lord
is work
that will reap
an eternal
(and temporary)
reward!*

"I owe, I owe, so off to work I go." Hmmm.
That's not exactly what God had in mind when
He instituted *work* in the Garden of Eden.

Adam's work was to reflect God's work. God
created the world from nothing; Adam was to
re-create the world using the materials
God gave him.

Since the Fall, we work against the curse.
But because of Christ, our work can again
bring joy. Find out how this week.

Work: from Tears to Cheers

Read
PSALM 126

If your work is just for a paycheck, you've received your reward.

Your World   It used to be called the rat race. But it's no longer a race for many. It's the "rat plod." Those rats slog along, barely able to keep their heads up, just wishing they could crawl back in bed and forget they exist.

The reason for the rat plod is the Fall. When Adam and Eve sinned in the Garden, God judged mankind. Since then our labors have been tangled with weeds, undergrowth, and frustration. The fruits of our labor have been produced with sweat, tears, toil, and blood.

God's Word   That's the bad news. Here's the good news: Faithfulness in work, though often frustrating, can bring great reward: "Those who sow in tears will reap with songs of joy. He who goes out weeping, carrying seed to sow, will return with songs of joy, carrying sheaves with him" (Psalm 126:5-6).

Your Walk   If the rewards for hard work done on earth were only heavenly, they would seem far away—pie in the sky, by and by. But God's rewards are not merely eternal. Better jobs, better salaries, and an inheritance for children are often His gifts in this world. To advance in our work can bring greater opportunities to advance His kingdom.

So keep working faithfully—even if you sometimes have to work in tears. His rewards—both temporal and eternal—are worth the effort!

Working with All Your Heart

Read
COLOSSIANS 3:22–4:1

Work with all your heart, and your heart will be in all your work.

Your World   You've probably heard it said that no matter what time you get to work, the first 15 minutes of the workday are yours. After all, there's coffee to drink, a newspaper to read, last night's television program to discuss.

I mean, priorities, please—right? Well, not quite. Christians should have a different set of priorities. And at the office or work site, our priority should be a full day's work for a full day's pay.

God's Word   The Scripture puts it this way: "Whatever you do, work at it with all your heart, as working for the Lord, not for men" (Colossians 3:23). Christians are responsible for doing their best. God doesn't want His people just yawning and punching the clock. No, He wants us to put our full effort into the work He's given us.

Christians are also responsible for doing their best with the right motive. No gritting the teeth, no grumbling. Why? Because we are to view all of our work, no matter what kind it is, as kingdom work.

Your Walk   Imagine that you walk into the boss's office on Monday morning for a scheduled meeting. But to your surprise, sitting in the boss's chair is the risen Christ. He looks at you, smiles, and says, "What's on the calendar this week?"

What do you think? Would you be more motivated to do your best for the remainder of the day?

143

Watching the Boss's Gaze

Read
MATTHEW 25:14-30

A job done for the Lord will certainly please your boss too.

Your World Ever wish you could put your feet up on your desk, sink back into your executive chair, and peruse the *Wall Street Journal* with a cup of coffee? Would you do it if you knew your boss could see you?

And what else would you avoid if you knew the boss was watching you? Perhaps taking a few extra minutes on lunch break? Coming in the back door a bit late in the morning?

God's Word We're not trying to pile on the guilt. But working solely for the boss's gaze has been a problem for a long time:

> Slaves, obey your earthly masters with respect and fear, and with sincerity of heart, just as you would obey Christ. Obey them not only to win their favor when their eye is on you, but like slaves of Christ, doing the will of God from your heart (Ephesians 6:5-6).

Christians don't work solely in the sight of the earthly boss. They serve the Lord, who sees all. So whether the boss is watching or not, they strive in their work for the same goal: their best.

Your Walk The way to rid our lives of BGS (Boss Gaze Syndrome) is to start working as if the Lord is our boss. (He is, you know.) We can do that, but only through prayer and trust in Him.

Determine today that you're the Lord's employee. If the earthly boss happens to notice, wonderful! But if not, rest in this: Christ notices and is pleased.

Working for Satisfaction

Read
NEHEMIAH 3

When you do your best, you please God, your boss, and you!

Your World   How should a Christian execute a job? With *skill*—for a fine, quality product. With *speed*—maximum efficiency for maximum output. With *sobriety*—for getting the day's work done right. With *satisfaction?* Absolutely.

God's Word   Solomon wrote, "Whatever your hand finds to do, do it with all your might, for in the grave, where you are going, there is neither working nor planning nor knowledge nor wisdom" (Ecclesiastes 9:10). In other words, do your best now; you won't have a chance later.

Now Solomon wasn't an atheist; he did believe in an afterlife. But he wrote much of Ecclesiastes as if there were no God, to show how meaningless life is apart from God.

But, according to Solomon, even the atheist finds some satisfaction in work. How much more, then, should the Christian. After all, his work reaps both a temporal and an eternal reward!

Your Walk   There's something wonderful in seeing a fine, finished product. Whether it's a pile of clean, folded clothes, a filing cabinet well-organized, or a rocket soon to blast off for Venus—there's real satisfaction in a job done "with all your might."

Why not approach your work that way today?

That Unreasonable Boss

Read
PROVERBS 29:2

*God has
His reasons
for giving
unreasonable
people authority.*

Your World What do you do when your boss is just plain nasty—the proverbial rotten egg? Do you try to get revenge? Do you find little ways to mess up his work and possibly get him demoted? Do you rail against him in the coffee room?

What's more, do you smile at his face, but when you have a chance, grimace to your crony in the desk behind him? Do you answer with a salute when he starts slinging orders, but then do the job barely up to spec?

God's Word The above examples, of course, exhibit a lot of hyperbole. But often we do find it next to impossible to give a bad boss our best. According to Peter, that reluctance is wrong: "Slaves, submit yourselves to your masters with all respect, not only to those who are good and considerate, but also to those who are harsh" (1 Peter 2:18).

Submit? Even if he's a modern-day slave driver? Yes.

Your Walk God has established authorities to represent Him in different spheres: in the family, in government, in labor, in the church. Our job is to submit graciously to those above us (even if they govern poorly) and to govern lovingly those under us (even if they submit poorly).

That's easier said than done. And God understands the difficulty. Center your life on the pursuit of knowing Christ, and He will help you do the impossible.

146

Not in Vain

Read
1 CORINTHIANS
15:57-58

*God's reward
for a job
well done
will last longer
than any raise
or promotion.*

No doubt about it, work is not easy. It's always time-consuming, sometimes oppressive, and frequently stressful. What's more, it's required.

Some people work as if there were no tomorrow. We call them workaholics. On the other hand, some people work as if there were an infinite amount of tomorrows in which to do today's work. We call them lazy.

How can we avoid the extremes? First, we should view work as a calling. We regularly speak of someone as called to the ministry, but rarely as called to the business world, the military, construction, science, or the arts. But God has prepared people to work for His kingdom in every sphere of human existence. In this way, His command to Adam to subdue the earth is fulfilled.

Second, we should practice the art of faithfulness. Faithfulness is firm resolve that hangs in there even when—no, *especially when*—it looks as if the odds are against us.

Third, we should remember that our work is meaningful to Christ. Christ is orchestrating His plan for the world as surely as J. S. Bach orchestrated the *Magnificat*. Your work, my work, every Christian's work plays a part in the symphony of history that Christ has already composed.

No wonder Paul said, "Your labor in the Lord is not in vain" (1 Corinthians 15:58).

Fresh Starts

Did you blow it last year? Last month? Last week? Do you wish you could just start over? Or maybe you fell into sin. Are you wondering if you can get back into a right relationship with God?

No one has ever needed a *fresh start* quite like King David. He really blew it. But today he is remembered as a man after God's own heart. How is that possible?

King David's prayer of repentance, Psalm 51, will be our topic in this section of readings. You will witness how, with God, a fresh start is more than just a resolution. It's a new heart and a new life.

God's Mercy and Fresh Starts

Read
2 SAMUEL 11:1-17

The same mercy that saves us restores us.

Your World   King David is the only person in the Bible called "a man after [God's] own heart" (1 Samuel 13:14). But this godly man had a weakness, and a stroll on his roof one spring evening (when all the other kings were leading their armies in battle) revealed that weakness.

He saw Bathsheba bathing. Not able to control the lust in his heart, he sent for her, lay with her, and she became pregnant. To cover his sin, he arranged for the murder of her husband, Uriah, one of his most loyal soldiers.

God's Word   King David seemed to be willing to live with his sins, but God sent Nathan the prophet to rebuke him (2 Samuel 12). As a result of this encounter, King David wrote Psalm 51. This psalm of confession and repentance is a prayer for God's mercy and a fresh start. "Have mercy on me, O God, according to your unfailing love; according to your great compassion blot out my transgressions" (Psalm 51:1).

Your Walk   A study of fresh starts goes hand in hand with a lesson on God's mercy. You can't have one without the other. And no one knew more about God's mercy and starting over than King David.

If you need a fresh start, whether due to sin or circumstances, ask God to give you the heart of King David—a man who exchanged misery for mercy, a man who wanted God's heart.

The Power of Confession

Read
2 SAMUEL 12:11-14

For him who confesses, shams are over and realities have begun.
—WILLIAM JAMES

Your World After Nathan's rebuke, David confessed, "I have sinned against the LORD" (2 Samuel 12:13). And though his confession was the first step in restoring his relationship with God and receiving His mercy, unfortunately, it could not change the consequences (2 Samuel 12:11-14).

God's Word No matter how much our sin affects other people, all sin is ultimately against God. And original sin cannot be used as an excuse, but instead makes us aware of our total depravity, and thus our need for God's mercy.

> Wash away all my iniquity and cleanse me from my sin. For I know my transgressions, and my sin is always before me. Against you, you only, have I sinned and done what is evil in your sight, so that you are proved right when you speak and justified when you judge. Surely I was sinful at birth, sinful from the time my mother conceived me (Psalm 51:2-5).

Your Walk Are you totally convinced of God's forgiveness in your life? If not, immediately ask God to show you what sins remain unconfessed and then confess them.

Remember that confessing your sins does not instantly take away your weaknesses in those areas. It can be a lifelong battle for some people. But part of God's mercy is to empower you to overcome any temptation (1 Corinthians 10:13) and to give you His strength where you are weak (2 Corinthians 12:9).

Opening the Inmost to the Utmost

Read
PSALM 51:6-9

God wants truth and wisdom in your inmost place because it is often filled with lies.

Your World Although his sins have been confessed and forgiven, King David continues his prayer of repentance. He bores deeper than the superficial sins of his confession to the core of his soul, "the inmost place."

He unlocks the door and hands God the key. He realizes this is necessary for God to be able to completely cleanse and heal him.

God's Word

Surely you desire truth in the inner parts; you teach me wisdom in the inmost place. Cleanse me with hyssop, and I will be clean; wash me, and I will be whiter than snow. Let me hear joy and gladness; let the bones you have crushed rejoice. Hide your face from my sins and blot out all my iniquity (Psalm 51:6-9).

Notice King David does not ask for joy or peace to indwell his inmost place. It seems that would have been much more pleasant. Instead, he submits to God's desire: truth and wisdom.

Your Walk Everyone has a secret "inmost place." It's a sacred spot where we keep our most precious dreams, emotions, and memories. Some of them are painful and require God's healing touch.

Is your "inmost place" off-limits to God? He will not go there without your permission.

What emotion or memory are you hiding in your "inmost place"? Keeping it locked up only prevents God from replacing your pain with His joy.

A Steadfast Spirit to Withstand Trials

Read
ZEPHANIAH 3:17

No spiritual earthquake can shake a steadfast spirit.

Your World   In certain cultures a thief was punished by having his hand cut off. What if King David had approached his sin this simply and gouged out his eyes? After all, his sin began with a lustful look.

King David understood that his body was not at the root of his sin. His heart was. He knew he needed a pure heart to keep his life pure. So he asked God to create one in him. He continues by asking for God's stabilizing strength to keep him from falling into sin again.

God's Word   Part of the beauty of God's mercy is that He uses our most bitter disappointments to teach us some of His sweetest lessons. If King David had not fallen into sin and repented, he may never have realized that his righteousness was dependent upon God, not himself.

> Create in me a pure heart, O God, and renew a steadfast spirit within me (Psalm 51:10).

Your Walk   Do you have a steadfast spirit? Steadfastness is built on your faith and knowledge that

- you belong to God;
- you are no longer unclean, but completely clean;
- you are free from judgment;
- you bring joy to God, He delights in you; and
- you can stop mourning over your sin and rejoice!

Ask God for a steadfast spirit today.

God's Promise to Restore

Read
GENESIS 28:15
ISAIAH 57:18-19

God's promise to restore gives us courage to draw closer to Him each day.

Your World As Psalm 51 progresses, so does King David's awareness of his need for God's presence and anointing. The once-arrogant, mighty warrior-king humbly cries out to God for help. In essence, the most powerful man on earth was admitting to God that he was powerless.

God's Word "Do not cast me from your presence or take your Holy Spirit from me. Restore to me the joy of your salvation and grant me a willing spirit, to sustain me" (Psalm 51:11-12).

Someone once said that King David didn't read Psalm 51, he lived it. He didn't have the advantage of a leather-bound Bible teeming with God's promises—not to mention concordances, outlines, and study notes. He prayed by raw faith, begging God not to leave Him.

Years later, King David would offer the same petition to God (Psalm 27:9) but then faithfully affirm, "Though my father and mother forsake me, the LORD will receive me" (verse 10).

Your Walk Are you aware that apart from God you are utterly powerless? (See John 15:5.) Are you willing, like King David, to prayerfully admit your helplessness to God and ask for His help?

God will never forsake you if you put your trust in Him. No matter what your past is like, He will restore in you the strength and joy you need to faithfully serve Him.

Fresh Starts

Read
PSALM 96

A restored soul can help bring other souls to God's restoration.

Over the past few years, we Christians have had to accept the hard fact that our leaders fail us, and many of us have been tempted to lose hope. Think about it: King David, a man after God's own heart, failed. And our contemporary leaders' respective sins pale in comparison to those of King David.

But just as King David was restored, our fallen leaders, if repentant, can be restored. And you, too, can be restored, for one purpose: new ministry to others. "Then I will teach transgressors your ways, and sinners will turn back to you. Save me from blood-guilt, O God, the God who saves me, and my tongue will sing of your righteousness" (Psalm 51:13-14).

As he concludes his prayer of repentance, King David understands he has a new ministry frontier stretching before him. Through his failures and subsequent repentance, he has gained new insight into the heart of God. He has experienced God's mercy and compassion, seen the horror of his sin, been cleansed to the core of his inner being, been restored to joy and gladness, and been given a new heart and a steadfast spirit.

Finally, King David is ready to minister to others.

What about you? Are you ready for a fresh start? No matter what you've done, God is waiting to give you a fresh start. Remember: It's more than just a new resolution—it's a new life.

*God
provided
the only way
of reconciliation
to Himself:
the cross.*

Reconciliation

Sin has pulled the universe apart.
It has separated us from God. From each other.
Even from ourselves.

"But God . . . " wrote the apostle Paul
(Ephesians 2:4 NKJV). And those two little words
are what the gospel is all about. Sin has pulled
the universe apart. But God has
reconciled the world to Himself.

This week, learn what the Bible says about
reconciliation and be drawn back to God, to
your loved ones, and to the inner harmony that
God intends for your life.

A Cure for Brokenness

Read
ROMANS 5:9-11

Be reconciled to God, and He will give you the rest you seek.

Your World Broken relationships. Broken promises. Broken marriages. Broken families. Broken hearts. Broken dreams. Broken trust. *Broken* is a word we use a lot, especially when we're describing people's relationships and commitments.

"Our hearts are restless until they find their rest in thee," St. Augustine said. Because of sin, our fundamental relationship—our relationship with God—is broken. As a result, we are restless. We have no peace. Our souls are missing that which they desire most. At the most basic level, we are barren, restless, broken.

God's Word But that's not the end of the story. The gospel is a healing message of reconciliation with the God whom we have so deeply offended.

The apostle Paul assured believers in Rome that all who place their faith in the reconciling work of Jesus Christ can be confident that their estrangement with God is over. "If, when we were God's enemies, we were reconciled to him through the death of his Son, how much more, having been reconciled, shall we be saved through his life!" (Romans 5:10).

Your Walk If you are a believer who doesn't feel reconciled to God, claim His promise of reconciliation today. Jesus Christ's righteousness carries more weight with God than your sins do. Pray that He would bring your feelings in line with His promises.

Reconciled with Each Other

Read
MATTHEW 5:21-26

*Let God's
reconciliation
flow from
your heart to
others.*

Your World As we saw yesterday, sin has estranged the human race from God. And as bad as that is, sin's horrible effects don't stop there. Sin also separates people from other people.

Because of sin, husbands are estranged from their wives to the degree that over 50 percent of American marriages end in divorce. Because of sin, mothers are estranged from their unborn babies to the degree that 1.5 million abortions occur annually in the United States alone. Because of sin, the crime rates of America's cities are skyrocketing, as people do violence to others made in God's image.

God's Word In the Sermon on the Mount, Jesus gives the solution to the enmity pitting brother against brother, race against race, nation against nation: Be reconciled to God, and then treat others the way God has treated you.

> If you are offering your gift at the altar and there remember that your brother has something against you, leave your gift there in front of the altar. First go and be reconciled to your brother; then come and offer your gift (Matthew 5:23-24).

Your Walk If there is someone with whom you have unresolved difficulties, call that person and get it resolved. Reconcile with him or her before you worship this weekend. Do that, and you'll be acting out the reconciliation that Christ purchased for you.

Out of the Slough of Despond

Read
PHILIPPIANS 4:6-7

Christ's people do not need to wallow in the mire of self-doubt.

Your World In *Pilgrim's Progress,* John Bunyan's classic allegory of the Christian life, Christian (the main character) finds himself drowning in a "Slough of Despond"—a metaphor for the overwhelming feelings of guilt and sinfulness at the core of people's souls. "As the sinner is awakened by his lost condition," Bunyan writes, "there arise in his soul many fears, doubts, and discouraging apprehensions, which get together and settle in this place; this is the reason for the badness of the ground." A remarkably insightful metaphor for the self-estrangement caused by sin, Bunyan's "Slough of Despond" is a place where feelings of fear and low self-esteem collect into an ugly and grotesque pool of self-doubt.

God's Word The gospel rescues people from the "Slough of Despond." The Son of God, who by His death reconciled us to His Father, offers us peace within ourselves—a peace the world is sadly missing. "Peace I leave with you; my peace I give you. I do not give to you as the world gives. Do not let your hearts be troubled and do not be afraid" (John 14:27).

Your Walk The best therapy for a troubled heart is the peace of God that passes all understanding. You can begin to find that peace as you meet God through the pages of His Word and through prayer. It also helps to seek the friendship, counsel, and prayers of your pastor, a professional, or a friend. And remember: Christ died to reconcile you with God and with yourself.

Hostility Between the Races

Read
EPHESIANS 2:11-22

There's no room in Christ's kingdom for racial bigotry.

Your World The hostility between the two races was deeply rooted in historical, cultural, and religious differences. Each race regarded the other as little more than dogs; neither race kept their feelings of hatred to themselves. The history of their conflict was an ugly tale of slavery, murder, infanticide, and prejudice.

This was the relationship between Jews and Gentiles in the ancient world.

God's Word The apostle Paul was a devout Jew. As a man of his culture, he would have regarded Gentiles as outside of God's salvation, strangers to the promises God delivered through Moses, hopelessly lost in idolatry.

But then everything changed. Paul was reconciled to God. And he realized that God had opened the boundaries of His mercy, reconciling people of every nation, language, and race. He explained his new way of thinking to the Christians in Ephesus: "His purpose was to create in himself one new man out of the two [races], thus making peace, and in this one body to reconcile both of them to God through the cross" (Ephesians 2:15-16).

Your Walk Unfortunately, believers have sometimes used the gospel to justify their culturally conditioned racial prejudice. And that is a dreadful shame.

If you harbor feelings of hatred based on race, follow Paul's example. Regard the reconciliation of Christ as the basis for racial reconciliation in your own heart.

Sharing the Message

Read
2 CORINTHIANS 5:16-21

*A robust
personal faith
in Christ
can never
be private.*

Your World "Martha," Joan said tentatively, "I'd like to ask you something. If you were to die today and God asked you, 'Why should I let you into My heaven?' what would you say?"

"Well, because I'm a good person," Martha said. "But to be honest, Joan, this conversation is making me uncomfortable. I know you're religious. I am, too, but my beliefs are very private."

God's Word Martha is like a lot of people in our culture. She believes that things deeply personal, such as faith, should be completely private. But to the apostle Paul, Christianity can never be limited to the private realm. Sharing the message of God's reconciling the world to Himself through Christ is the most important task (and privilege) in the Christian life:

> All this is from God, who reconciled us to himself through Christ and gave us the ministry of reconciliation: that God was reconciling the world to himself in Christ, not counting men's sins against them. And he has committed to us the message of reconciliation. We are therefore Christ's ambassadors, as though God were making his appeal through us. We implore you on Christ's behalf: Be reconciled to God (2 Corinthians 5:18-20).

Your Walk Sharing the gospel is sometimes uncomfortable these days. But doing so now is no less essential than it ever was. Our faith is deeply personal, but never private. Share Christ with someone today.

Imagine

Read
COLOSSIANS 1:15-23

*Jesus' work
on the cross
paves the way
for a new world
reconciled
to God.*

Imagine a world fully reconciled to God. It would be radically different from the world you live in.

- Your neighbors would be kind and friendly, always willing to help each other.
- Your children would obey you willingly and happily.
- Your relationships would be free from conflict.
- Your work would be unencumbered by the strains and stresses of sin.
- Your church would be packed every weekend with worshipers.

Sounds great, doesn't it?

Scripture promises that such a time is coming. In fact, the apostle Paul envisions a time when the work Christ performed on the cross will effect a cosmic reconciliation—a universe brought back to God. "God was pleased to have all his fullness dwell in [Christ], and through him to reconcile to himself all things, whether things on earth or things in heaven, by making peace through his blood, shed on the cross" (Colossians 1:19-20).

If you're a believer, God has made peace with you by awakening your heart to your sin and His holiness. But that's just a foretaste of the reconciliation to come, which will be completed when Jesus returns in power and glory.

As you worship this weekend, imagine the glory of the reconciled world to come. And resolve to share the message of reconciliation more faithfully with your unsaved friends, family members, and associates.

Gratitude

If you've ever received an unexpected gift,
you know what *gratitude* feels like.
And you know how you responded:
with spontaneous thanks.

When we consider what God
has done for us—giving us the unexpected
and cherished gift of His love—our hearts
should respond with gratitude that flows out
into lives of service to Him. In your quiet times
this week, be grateful to Him for your salvation
as you explore the psalmist's gratitude.

A Song of Gratitude

Read
PSALM 136

God is good to us despite our sin. For that we should be grateful.

Your World An attitude of gratitude is contagious. Someone who has a positive attitude about life makes other people feel good about life as well. Unfortunately, the opposite is also true. Negative people breed negativity in those they come in contact with.

Believers have struggles in life. The world, the sinful nature, and the devil make life difficult even for—especially for—the most sanctified Christians. But of all people, believers have reason to be filled with gratitude. God has created us and drawn us to Himself. That's reason enough to . . . sing!

God's Word Psalm 136 is a song of gratitude. And though the psalm was written thousands of years ago, the principles that led the psalmist to gratitude are supremely relevant in today's world.

The primary reason we should be grateful is that God has forgiven our sins. He has treated us mercifully, in a way we don't deserve. "Oh, give thanks to the LORD, for He is good! For His mercy endures forever. . . . Oh, give thanks to the God of heaven! For His mercy endures forever" (Psalm 136:1, 26 NKJV).

Your Walk Because Psalm 136 is a divinely inspired song of gratitude, we're going to focus our thoughts on this portion of God's Word this week. As you reflect on the history of God's ways in the history of His people, reflect on the things He has done in your life. And be grateful.

Grateful for His Lordship

Read
PSALM 136:2-3

Those who worship the true God should sing with joyful gratitude.

Your World   There are many gods competing for people's allegiance in today's world:

- Allah, the god of Islam, can claim the adoration of millions of adherents, several nations, and rapidly growing numbers throughout the world.
- The thousands of gods in the pantheon of Hinduism receive veneration from millions, especially in India and surrounding nations.
- The universe is god in many Hindu-influenced sects.
- The self is god to many New Age organizations.

God's Word   Though there are many false gods, there is only one true God. Only He is truly Lord. Only He has the power to determine all things that come to pass. And we should be supremely grateful that the true God, the Lord, has called us to be His people.

In the words of the psalmist, "Oh, give thanks to the God of gods! For His mercy endures forever. Oh, give thanks to the Lord of lords! For His mercy endures forever" (Psalm 136:2-3 NKJV).

Your Walk   As a Christian, you are a member of a blessed company. God has placed you in the body of His beloved Son, and that is cause for rejoicing.

The next time you are tempted to grumble about your circumstances, give thanks to the Lord of lords! His mercy endures forever, and there's no better reason in all the world to be grateful.

Gratitude Toward the Creator

Read
PSALM 136:4-9

*Nature sings
a song of
gratitude
to its Creator.*

Your World "What makes the Supreme Being different from a human being?" theologian R. C. Sproul asks.

Notice that both concepts share a common word, *being*. When we say that God is the supreme Being, we are saying that He is a being who differs in kind from other ordinary beings. What precisely is that difference? He is called supreme because He has no beginning. He is supreme because all other beings owe their existence to Him, and He owes His existence to none other than Himself. He is the eternal Creator. Everything else is the work of His creation.

God's Word God's creative works are all worthy of praise, regardless of their size. Whether looming over the horizon or teeming under the lens of a microscope, God's creation marvels us and leads us to grateful praise.

To Him who alone does great wonders, for His mercy endures forever; to Him who by wisdom made the heavens, for His mercy endures forever; to Him who laid out the earth above the waters, for His mercy endures forever; to Him who made great lights, for His mercy endures forever (Psalm 136:4-7 NKJV).

Your Walk This week, take a walk and marvel at God's creation. Rejoice in the beauty and diversity of life God has created. Lift your heart to Him and say, "Thank You, God. I am grateful for the beauty of Your creation—a beauty that reflects Your beauty."

Grateful to Our Redeemer

Read
PSALM 136:10-16

Released from the bondage of sin, let us be grateful to our Redeemer.

Your World In his book *Knowing the Truth of God's Love,* Peter Kreeft writes,

The love of God is a timeless truth, an eternal fact about God, the essence of God, the life of the Trinity, what God is. But once God creates a world of time, this timeless truth becomes also a temporal truth. This love becomes a love story. Like white light refracted through a prism and split into many colors, God's eternal love-nature, expressed through the prism of time, becomes God's multi-colored love-story. History is His story.

God's Word The psalmist calls us to be grateful for God's love story. In Jewish history, one event rose above all others as the supreme act of God's redeeming His people: the Exodus.

To Him who divided the Red Sea in two . . . and made Israel pass through the midst of it . . . but overthrew Pharaoh and his army in the Red Sea . . . to Him who led His people through the wilderness, for His mercy endures forever (Psalm 136:13-16 NKJV).

Your Walk The Exodus has its new covenant counterpart: the cross. And just as the Old Testament saints were to show God gratitude for His redeeming act, we should express our undying gratitude to God for redeeming us from our own Egypt: our sin.

Imagine yourself released from bondage and brought through the Red Sea. Your redemption is far greater than that. Give God appropriate thanks.

Grateful for God's Protection

Read
PSALM 136:17-24

*Give thanks
to the Lord,
for He delivers
us from all
our enemies.*

Your World In our spiritual lives, we face great enemies. We face the enemy of our own nature, which continually desires to satisfy itself rather than God. We face the enmity of the world, which wickedly desires to lead us into temptation. And we face the enmity of the devil, who, as God's sworn enemy, attacks those who have pledged themselves to Christ. Those are formidable enemies waiting to attack us at all times and in all places.

God's Word But God doesn't leave us at the mercy of our enemies, and for that we must follow the example of the psalmist and give Him grateful praise.

> To Him who struck down great kings . . . and gave their land as a heritage . . . a heritage to Israel His servant . . . who remembered us in our lowly state . . . and rescued us from our enemies, for His mercy endures forever (Psalm 136:17, 21-24 NKJV).

Your Walk "Personal mercies awake the sweetest song," Charles Spurgeon wrote. On a card small enough to fit in your wallet, write down ten great things God has done for you.

Whenever you are tempted to feel ungrateful for the circumstances in your life, pull out that card and meditate on it. Contemplate the good things God has done, and you'll remember that God is more powerful than whatever problem you face.

Your Response

Read
PSALM 136

Gratitude for God's good works should be our continuous attitude.

During the time of the Arian controversy in the church, Athanasius, bishop of Alexandria, was the most powerful defender of the orthodox truth concerning Christ's deity. The heretic Arius, who boasted many followers, claimed Jesus was merely God's first creature, rather than God come to earth as a man.

The controversy turned violent. Syrianus and his troops assaulted Athanasius in his church one night. Many were wounded and some killed. But Athanasius was calm. During a service following the attack, he directed the deacon to begin singing, "Give thanks to the Lord for He is good. . . ." The congregation spontaneously responded, "For His mercy endures forever!"

This week we have reflected on the fact that God gives us reason to be grateful toward Him—to give Him thanks for the merciful way He deals with us in our lives. But such knowledge is worthless without our response—without life change.

In the weeks to come, remember what you've learned from Psalm 136: Give thanks. Be grateful. Acknowledge to God His good leading in your life. Praise Him for guiding your circumstances for your good.

Even if you can't see God in your present situation, He is there. He is with you. You can trust Him. You can be grateful to Him, knowing that He does all things well, including the things going on in your life right now.

Leisure

Ah, vacation time.
The days spent on vacation are
the most fun, relaxing days of the year,
aren't they? Or are they?

To some, *leisure* is the purpose of life itself.
We call these people "goof-offs." To others,
leisure is merely an extension of work.
We call these people "workaholics."
Is there a middle ground?

This week, search God's Word for
God's view on leisure. And have fun!

Is Leisure Time Spiritual?

Read
DEUTERONOMY 6:4-9

*Leisure is
God's gift
to busy souls.
Have fun
to His glory!*

Your World   Some years ago a study conducted by *Time* magazine produced some statistics on what people do with their leisure time. The activities included watching television, reading newspapers, listening to music, jogging, reading books, gardening, playing golf, and more.

Unfortunately, nothing connected with the spiritual realm was mentioned. That raises this question: Should leisure be in some sense spiritual?

God's Word   In the apostle Paul's view, nothing is exempt from God's authority: "Whether you eat or drink or whatever you do, do it all for the glory of God" (1 Corinthians 10:31).

Everything in life, whether it's leisure time, work time, or worship time, is to be done to the glory of God.

Your Walk   Does that mean you can never relax? Certainly not. God relaxed by instituting the Sabbath after He had created the universe.

Does that mean your reading the paper or listening to music should glorify God? Certainly.

The next time you read the newspaper to relax, give God praise when you read a feature that makes you laugh. When you read about a tragedy, ask God to have mercy on the people involved.

Whether you read, listen, lift, bat, swing, sail, snooze, throw, call, fly, run, or fish for leisure, remember this: Nothing is too insignificant to glorify God.

In Desperate Need of Rest

Read
PSALM 19

Rest your body and soul by enjoying the Creator's creation.

Your World Joe Harris, director of communications at a small but successful company, stepped into his office and looked at his appointment book.

Scheduled for the day were three meetings, a project due to the company president, a tour of the company by a group of students, and an interview with an influential business magazine—all before the first of two luncheons! Is it any wonder that Joe's wife tells him he needs to relax?

God's Word God understands the problem well. In fact, in one case His antidote for some "burned-out" disciples was rest and relaxation:

> The apostles gathered around Jesus and reported to him all they had done and taught. Then, because so many people were coming and going that they did not even have a chance to eat, he said to them, "Come with me by yourselves to a quiet place and get some rest" (Mark 6:30-31).

Your Walk God doesn't reduce life to the drudgery of unending activity—even if the activity is, like evangelism, vital.

When leisure is a change of activity, it can recharge your batteries by giving rest to your brain and body.

Planning a fun-filled trip to Disney World this year? If your life is already full of mind-and-body-numbing activity, you might consider pitching a hammock in your backyard instead.

175

Leisure Is Not Idleness

Read
PROVERBS
10:4; 13:4

Spending your leisure time helping others is a gift both to you and to them.

Your World Leisure is not necessarily idleness. The dictionary defines it as "time free from work or duties."

With our leisure time, we sometimes can accomplish as much or more than in our working hours. The pleasure of leisure time is in doing something different, something refreshing, something that does not carry the stress of normal activity.

God's Word The writer of Proverbs spoke of the "excellent woman" and how she used her leisure time: "She watches over the affairs of her household and does not eat the bread of idleness. Her children arise and call her blessed; her husband also, and he praises her" (Proverbs 31:27-28).

Why did the woman's husband praise her? Because she did things beyond her normal responsibilities that brought her pleasure and prosperity: She bought a field, planted a vineyard, extended her hands to the poor. This woman used her leisure time to serve.

Your Walk Not all leisure calls for service or giving. But Christians need to think of leisure time as a chance to help other people.

We don't want to wear ourselves out with extra duties, but being a volunteer at the hospital, helping in a rescue mission, or visiting shut-ins can be healthy and joyful ways to serve, to do something different, to find that change of pace that refreshes.

You Can Get Satisfaction

Read
ECCLESIASTES 2:24-26

*The future
will still come
if you take time
to enjoy
the present.*

Your World   Years ago, Mick Jagger of the Rolling Stones sang, "I can't get no satisfaction." What a commentary on our age. Though we have more pleasures, more leisure time, more things to do, and more places to go, real satisfaction seems to elude us. Why?

Perhaps it's because we tend to focus exclusively on what could be (the future), rather than enjoy what is (the present).

God's Word   The writer of Ecclesiastes voiced wise counsel about experiencing satisfaction in life and making the most of our leisure time (two principles that go together): "A man can do nothing better than to eat and drink and find satisfaction in his work. This too, I see, is from the hand of God" (Ecclesiastes 2:24).

What did the writer mean? God's good gifts—eating, drinking, working, experiencing His creation—are meant to satisfy, to give joy. In other words, when we're sitting down to dinner, we're not to be preoccupied with what we're going to do later in the evening. Instead, we need to concentrate on this bite of green beans and that piece of conversation. We're to experience the present fully.

Your Walk   Is your leisure time gone before you've enjoyed it? Could it be that even during times of rest, you're so preoccupied with what might happen tomorrow that you can't enjoy today?

Using Your Time Wisely

Read
EPHESIANS 5:1-21

*Don't forget:
Use your time
wisely, and
you will
grow wiser
in time.*

Your World A great Chinese philosopher said, "Doing nothing is better than being busy doing nothing." Unfortunately, that proverb pegs what some people of the modern world seem to be so busily occupied with: selfish, meaningless pursuits. In other words, nothing.

God's Word Perhaps our tendency is to use times of leisure in empty pursuits, rather than in godly, fun-filled rest and refreshment.

Perhaps the apostle Paul understood that psychology when he wrote, "Be very careful, then, how you live—not as unwise but as wise, making the most of every opportunity, because the days are evil" (Ephesians 5:15-16).

When Paul challenges us to make the most of every opportunity, he does not mean, "Thou shalt not relax or have fun." But he does mean that we shouldn't waste our time—even our leisure time.

Your Walk Take a hard look at what you do in your time off. Are you being "wise" in your use of that time? Are you giving yourself a real change of activity from your work? Maybe you need to use the time to build a relationship, to love, to grow in Christ, to serve, to just rest.

An excellent way to spend some of your leisure time this evening would be to relax in the Lord. Tell Him you love Him and want to be the best you can be for Him.

Time to Think

Read
PHILIPPIANS 4

Make leisure time praise time as you think about God's mighty works and marvelous deeds.

Don Herold, famous cartoonist, once said,

> If today's average American is confronted with an hour of leisure, he is likely to palpitate with panic. An hour without anything to do? He jumps into a car and drives off fiercely in pursuit of diversion. We need less leg action, and more acute observation, as we go. Slow down the muscle and stir up the mind.

And what should our minds be thinking about? "Finally, brothers, whatever is true, whatever is noble, whatever is right, whatever is pure, whatever is lovely, whatever is admirable—if anything is excellent or praiseworthy—think about such things" (Philippians 4:8).

One reason God gives us leisure time is so we can have time to reflect on Him and His world. We can think about anything and everything: the beautiful, the noble, the good, the fun, the important, the not-so-important. A memory. An idea. A plan. A deed. A work of God. The beauty of a lilac. The magnificent inner workings of a watch.

Take pleasure in a child's smile, a teenager's song, a grandfather's joke. All of these are God's gifts. To partake of the fullness of life and make the most of the little things is a big part of what life is all about. If you find yourself wondering what to do with your leisure time, sit down and think about the Lord, about His world, about your life.

Let your leisure lead to praise.

*Tolerance
practices
civility.
It doesn't
scream
at those
who disagree.*

Tolerance

Tolerance is a democratic tradition.
Because we love freedom, we allow all points
of view to be civilly accorded their day in the
court of public opinion.

But the noble tradition of tolerance is
threatened in our day. With increasing
frequency, all points of view are tolerated except
religiously motivated ones—particularly if the
religion doing the motivating is
biblical Christianity.

In your quiet times this week, explore the
Christian foundation of tolerance. And pray
that this foundation would survive the
attacks of the intolerant and the uncivil.

Two Cheers for Tolerance

Read
MATTHEW
13:24-29; 36-43

Principled tolerance acts with civility toward all— even those with opposing viewpoints.

Your World In a sense, the people of ancient Israel had it easy. There wasn't much guesswork in drawing the line between right and wrong, legal and illegal, accepted and forbidden. The culture of ancient Israel was a divinely-inspired one. The people officially granted their submission to God. They used His revealed law as their "Constitution."

Not so in our pluralistic society.

God's Word When Rome ruled the world, the apostle Paul didn't exhort Christians to impose God's law on an unbelieving public. Instead, he encouraged believers to promote peace and the gospel: "I urge . . . that requests, prayers, intercession and thanksgiving be made for everyone—for kings and all those in authority, that we may live peaceful and quiet lives in all godliness and holiness" (1 Timothy 2:1-2).

Your Walk Unlike the ancient Israelites, we live in a society that doesn't recognize God's right to rule. We must live and work with civility among people whose value systems and religious beliefs are often the opposite of ours. At the same time we are to be light and salt, never compromising the truth God has revealed in his Word.

The line separating what we should tolerate from what we shouldn't can be difficult to draw, but it's not impossible. This week we'll glean principles from Scripture we can apply even in this highly pluralistic world as we await God's perfect society.

Tolerance Gives Time for Repentance

Read
ECCLESIASTES 3:8

God is patient with sinners, wanting all to come to repentance.

Your World You can almost hear Him quietly sighing as He turns; you can almost see Him gently shaking His head as He speaks.

Jesus was traveling through Samaria to Jerusalem to celebrate the Feast of Tabernacles. When it began to get dark, Jesus called two of His followers and sent them into a nearby village to request shelter for the entourage.

But Samaritans were commonly hostile to Jews—especially Jews traveling to Jerusalem during religious feasts. These villagers displayed their hostility by refusing hospitality to the travelers.

God's Word "When the disciples James and John saw this, they asked, 'Lord, do you want us to call fire down from heaven to destroy them?' But Jesus turned and rebuked them" (Luke 9:54-55).

Jesus didn't come to destroy; He came to save. Because salvation was (and is) His primary mission, He was patient with sinners—even those who snubbed Him.

Your Walk Jesus lived in a mixed culture. So do we. As in His day, our world consists of solid Bible believers, the nominally religious, and thoroughgoing pagans.

Imitate Jesus. Be passionate for righteousness. Never condone sin. But remember: The time is not yet at hand for a world in which righteousness fully dwells. So be patient with your unbelieving friends in the interest of their salvation.

The Price of Freedom

Read
JOHN 8:32

When truth is set free, it sets people free.

Your World Freedom is highly valued in America. And because tolerance of varying viewpoints is a necessary means of preserving freedom for all, tolerance is highly valued as well.

Americans tolerate their neighbors' ideas, speech, worship, and choice of friends as long as their neighbors' actions don't violate the freedom of others. As believers, then, we sometimes must make some concessions to the secular society so that we might have the freedom to protect and propagate truth.

God's Word Doing so has biblical precedent. The prophet Daniel was a captive of Babylon. He was given a new name: "The chief official gave them new names: to Daniel, the name Belteshazzar" (Daniel 1:7).

Daniel's new name meant "Bel, protect his life." In other words, the name was idolatrous. But having a false god's name didn't prevent Daniel from worshiping the true God, so Daniel tolerated it. Only when he was ordered to disobey God did Daniel draw the line (see chapter 3).

Your Walk Intolerance of sin is vital. Christians must be firm. For example, you can't tolerate homosexuals or so-called sex-education experts infecting your child's mind with their "values-free" poison. We cannot ever condone what the Bible calls sin.

But choose your battles wisely. And fight them with civility. When someone is trying to impose sin on you or other people, fight for truth. At other times, the wiser course may be to practice quiet discourse.

When "Tolerance" Is Intolerance

Read
PSALM 12:8

Tolerance allows freedom of religion; intolerance demands freedom from offense.

Your World Many people today have forgotten that tolerance is a necessary means for preserving freedom *of* expression. Instead, they reason that tolerance requires freedom *from* anything that might be deemed offensive.

So in the name of tolerance, a public-school teacher isn't free to keep a Bible on his or her desk in the classroom. Why? The nonreligious might be offended.

God's Word One tremendous value of the tolerance of American society is freedom of religious expression. Believers haven't always had such freedom. The religious rulers of the apostles' day were intolerant of the gospel: "They called [Peter and John] in again and commanded them not to speak or teach at all in the name of Jesus" (Acts 4:18).

Your Walk The American tradition of protecting religious freedom is waning. Many insist on freedom of expression while denying that same freedom to those who base their expression on biblical values. And that is hypocrisy.

Don't mistake tyranny for tolerance. Freedom *of* religion is not at all the same thing as freedom *from* religion. The writers of the U.S. Constitution protected the former. Pray that God would frustrate the efforts of those who would remove that protection.

Tolerance in the Church

Read
ROMANS 14:1-13

In essentials, unity; in nonessentials, liberty; in all things, charity.

Your World "Charles, it's obvious that you love the Lord," said Bill, one of Charles's closest friends. "But why is it that your church baptizes babies?"

"Because we see baptism as similar to circumcision," Charles said. "And Abraham was told to circumcise his whole family when he believed. Why is it that your church doesn't baptize your children?"

"Because we see baptism as only for believers," Bill said, "and therefore inappropriate for those who aren't old enough to give a profession of faith."

Bill and Charles smiled at each other and agreed to disagree agreeably.

God's Word Discussions on biblically questionable topics have occurred continually for almost 2000 years. Unfortunately, such discussions haven't always ended so amicably.

But according to the apostle Paul, believers ought to be tolerant of people who take different positions on topics the Bible doesn't clearly settle: "Let us stop passing judgment on one another" (Romans 14:13).

Your Walk Many topics are highly controversial in the church. And on some of those—especially matters that are clear subjects of Scripture—the church must stand unwaveringly. But when Bible-believing Christians have made little progress in coming to a consensus on a subject after centuries of discussion, tolerance is the best approach. When Jesus comes back, He'll settle the controversies once and for all.

Tolerant Truth

Read
PSALM 119:30

To know truth and not accept it does not nullify it.

The late professor Allan Bloom opened his bestselling book, *The Closing of the American Mind,* with the following sentence: "There is one thing a professor can be absolutely certain of: Almost every student entering the university believes, or says he believes, that truth is relative." In other words, American college students dogmatically believe that nothing—absolutely nothing—is true at all times and in all places.

Professor Bloom goes on to write that American students' relativism is the result of a twisted view of tolerance. According to this twisted tolerance, tolerating other points of view requires believing that no point of view is actually true.

Nothing could be further from the truth. God's truth, revealed in His Word and in the world He made, transcends time, place, and situation because the God of truth transcends time, place, and situation. Jesus was by no means a relativist: "Sanctify them by the truth; your word is truth" (John 17:17), Jesus prayed to His Father.

Mankind will only know the full revelation of truth at Christ's Second Coming. Until then, we realize that other people have the same right that we do to express ideas, opinions, and beliefs. But we don't kid ourselves that all opinions are equally true.

If you know Jesus Christ, you know Him who is the truth. Practice the tolerance of civility and Christian charity in His name, but proclaim His truth.

*God wants
His people
to depend
on Him—
and on each
other.*

Dependability

You're on the side of a cliff,
climbing foot by foot. Suddenly a hand
reaches out to yours, helping you up.

At times, life is like climbing a mountain.
You wouldn't want to face the ups and downs
without someone to help you get to the top.
You're a member of a team. Your teammates
depend on you; you depend on them.

The Bible has a lot to say about the
importance of *dependability*. Explore
its message in your quiet times this week.

The Depend- ability of God

Read
PSALM 20:7

One word describes how we should react to God's dependability: trust.

Your World "God said it, I believe it, and that settles it." So reads a bumper sticker popular among Christians.

To some unbelievers that message typifies Christianity at its worst. Such blind acceptance of absolute authority is the opposite of their idea of freedom.

But that kind of confidence in God isn't blind; it's based on good evidence. God has demonstrated in the Scriptures and in our experience that He always tells the truth.

God's Word When God makes a promise, He keeps it. He is dependable. We can trust Him completely.

According to the apostle Paul, because God so dependably has done what He has pledged, we can plan our lives with confidence—the kind of confidence that comes from keeping His promises in mind. "Since we have these promises, dear friends, let us purify ourselves from everything that contaminates body and spirit, perfecting holiness out of reverence for God" (2 Corinthians 7:1).

Your Walk Because of God's perfect dependability, you can trust that He will bless your efforts—

- to share the truth about His Son with your unbelieving friends, colleagues, and relatives;
- to plan your finances for you and your children's futures;
- to obey Him in all situations—even when the cost is high.

The Blessings of Dependability

Read
1 CORINTHIANS 4:2

When the going gets tough, the dependable keep going.

Your World A person may have supreme intelligence, terrific looks, enormous talent, and athletic prowess, yet accomplish little. How? Through a lack of that simple but necessary quality for success: dependability. Those who lack dependability have a tough time dealing with the inevitable trials of life.

God's Word The Word of God is about truth. And truth isn't limited to our thoughts. Our emotions are subject to truth. And so Scripture contains sections that stir our hearts to love the truths God reveals to us. Likewise, our actions must bow before truth, and so Scripture is often intensely practical.

Here's a practical truth in any era: People who dependably do God's will, will be rewarded.

> Lazy hands make a man poor, but diligent hands bring wealth. He who gathers crops in summer is a wise son, but he who sleeps during harvest is a disgraceful son (Proverbs 10:4-5).

In this contrast, "diligent hands"—in other words, dependability at work—produce physical blessings; lazy hands produce nothing.

Your Walk You're probably concerned about the future. Dependably working at your calling is the surest way to secure a stable future for you and your children.

The next time you're tempted to give up on God's work, remember: Dependable hands bring God's blessing.

Your Children Are Counting on You

Read
1 TIMOTHY 3:4-5

*Parents
who depend
on Christ have
children who
can depend
on them.*

Your World Amy Carmichael had over 100 children—and she never married!

Don't worry. It isn't a scandal worthy of a tabloid headline. Amy Carmichael was a missionary to India. Remaining single all her life, Amy founded the Dohnavur Fellowship, a home for hundreds of children who were rescued from the slavery of Hindu temple prostitution.

Amy's children counted on her for their very lives, and she dependably prayed for and provided for them. God richly blessed her efforts with countless lives saved, and almost as many souls saved.

God's Word God gives children as a gift. And in the divine order of things, children, especially when they are young, depend almost entirely on their parents.

As a result, God expects parents to faithfully care for and provide for their children, using God's perfect dependability as an example. "He who brings trouble on his family will inherit only wind, and the fool will be servant to the wise" (Proverbs 11:29).

Your Walk If you have children, they are counting on you. They depend on you. They look to you for physical, emotional, and spiritual guidance.

Give your children what they need. Dependably provide for them, pray for them, and pass on your wisdom to them. They'll inherit much more than wind; they'll inherit your best.

Your Spouse Is Counting on You

Read
1 PETER 3:8-9

When spouses can depend on each other, there is mutual submission.

Your World Jim and Linda just celebrated their twelfth wedding anniversary. But it hasn't been easy.

Eight years ago, they almost divorced. In the painful process, they became Christians. And the Lord saved more than their souls; He saved their marriage.

Both Jim and Linda changed their lives as God changed their hearts. Jim's primary earthly concern became being the husband God wanted him to be. Likewise, Linda searched the Scriptures for truth about her responsibilities and privileges as a wife. As Jim and Linda began to depend more on each other, they gained a new and exciting intimacy.

God's Word Spouses count on each other for many of life's most basic necessities and pleasures. And so, good husbands and wives dependably give their hearts, minds, and bodies to their spouses to provide for their needs: "Each man should have his own wife, and each woman her own husband. The husband should fulfill his marital duty to his wife, and likewise the wife to her husband" (1 Corinthians 7:2-3).

Your Walk Read 1 Corinthians 13:1-7, Ephesians 5:21-33, and Colossians 3:18-19—passages that give instruction on how to treat your spouse with love. Then pray that God would empower you to be the person on whom your spouse can depend for the love and support he or she needs.

When People Are Undepend-able

Read
ACTS 15:36-41

Those who lack dependability shouldn't expect the rewards of faithfulness.

Your World   "I've had it!" barked Mr. Wilson to the manager of client services. "We almost lost the J & J Real Estate account because we can't depend on MacIntyre to follow up properly. I don't care how good a salesman he is. If he blows one more account by being undependable, fire him!"

God's Word   Undependable people shouldn't expect to be tolerated forever. And that's not merely a principle of modern business.

Mark (the author of the second gospel, according to many scholars) deserted the apostle Paul during his first missionary journey. When Mark wanted to accompany Paul on his second journey, Paul said no. "Barnabas wanted to take John, also called Mark, with them, but Paul did not think it wise to take him, because he had deserted them in Pamphylia and had not continued with them in the work" (Acts 15:37-38).

Your Walk   How's your follow-through? Are you like Paul (who could always be counted on) or Mark (who deserted the cause before it was finished)?

Earnestly seek to follow through on your commitments. And then rejoice in this: Because of the work of Christ on your behalf, God will not only help you become more dependable, but will also forgive your mistakes.

And don't worry about Mark. He became one of Paul's most dependable helpers (see 2 Timothy 4:11).

Trust

Read
JOHN 14:6

Jesus is the ultimate Truth, sent by the Author of all truth.

Trust.

Dependable people are trustworthy. You can count on them. They do what they say they are going to do; they don't do what they say they are not going to do. And though no mere human in this world is completely trustworthy, one man lived a life of thorough dependability: the God-man, Jesus Christ.

"I tell you the truth, no one can see the kingdom of God unless he is born again" (John 3:3). A hard saying, but uttered by One whose words are utterly dependable. Do you trust Him?

"I tell you the truth, whoever hears my word and believes him who sent me has eternal life and will not be condemned; he has crossed over from death to life" (John 5:24). A word of encouragement for all those who will come to Jesus. Do you trust Him?

"If you do not believe that I am the one I claim to be, you will indeed die in your sins" (John 8:24). A word of warning for all those who refuse His call. Do you trust Him?

"I am the way and the truth and the life. No one comes to the Father except through me" (John 14:6). A self-description that should cause every trusting heart to leap and every unbelieving heart to fear. Do you trust Him?

Jesus is the only way to God, the utterly dependable One, the Source of eternal life. Trust Him this weekend by giving Him your whole heart in worship.

Life's Issues

*It is
impossible
to mentally
and socially
enslave those
whose freedom
is in Christ.*

Freedom

Freedom is a precious concept in today's world. The right to choose apart from the coercion of other people is a fundamental value in democracies.

But even freedom has its limits. And when freedom becomes license, it enslaves. It entangles. It runs roughshod over the freedom of others.

This week, explore how Jesus Christ liberates believers from the judgments of other people and the prison of sin. And rejoice in Him who has made you free indeed.

Freedom from Falsehood

Read
JOHN 8:31-38

When freedom loosens itself from truth, freedom becomes bondage.

Your World "You born-again Christians are so narrow-minded," Judy said angrily to Bill in the conference room, where a break in the morning meeting had turned into a heated discussion on homosexuality.

"You read an ancient book and think you have a monopoly on truth," she continued. "Instead of trying to impose your 'truth' on everybody else, why don't you let people be free to follow their own desires?"

God's Word Judy suffers from a common misconception: She thinks freedom and absolute truth are incompatible. But according to Jesus, nothing could be further from the truth. In fact, true freedom depends on truth:

> If you hold to my teaching, you are really my disciples. Then you will know the truth, and the truth will set you free (John 8:31-32).

Your Walk To many people in our society, freedom means total license. In other words, to be free you can't be restrained by any external authority—even the authority of truth.

But in the Bible, freedom means something completely different from license. Biblical freedom is the ability to live according to, rather than apart from, truth.

As you read this book and your Bible this week, ask God to teach you more of His truth—the truth that sets people truly free.

200

Our Freedom in Christ

Read
ROMANS 6:15-23

Because of Christ, sin no longer has dominion over us.

Your World   In *Pilgrim's Progress*, John Bunyan's seventeenth-century allegory about the Christian faith, our freedom in Christ is vividly pictured. A man named Christian is oppressed by a terrible, debilitating burden on his back. He must carry the enslaving burden everywhere he goes.

Christian lugs his burden through life, searching for a way out of his bondage. Finally, when he reaches the wicket gate surrounding the cross, he lays down his burden and begins life anew.

God's Word   The message of *Pilgrim's Progress* is clear: There is only one solution for the sin that enslaves us. That solution is Jesus Christ.

The apostle Paul, writing to the church in Rome, made clear that faith in Christ gives believers freedom from the oppressive burden of sin:

> Thanks be to God that, though you used to be slaves to sin, you wholeheartedly obeyed the form of teaching to which you were entrusted. You have been set free from sin and have become slaves to righteousness (Romans 6:17-18).

Your Walk   Christ won victory over sin on the cross. As a result, you now enjoy freedom from the penalty and power of sin. You will one day enjoy freedom from the very presence of sin.

Rejoice that God has set you free, and look forward with anticipation to the day when Christ returns to make your freedom perfect and complete.

Freedom Versus Legalism

Read
GALATIANS 5:1

Commitment to God's Word is freedom from the judgment of others.

Your World   "I'll tell you why I don't go to church," James said to Philip, his next-door neighbor, after Philip had invited him to church. "Twenty years ago, I was kicked out of church because I refused to cut my long hair. But when one of the leaders in the church was caught having an affair, he was allowed to stay. In fact, he remained a church leader. That seems like hypocrisy to me."

God's Word   Freedom in Christ isn't freedom from God's unchanging moral law. But it is freedom from the arbitrary cultural strictures of others—even other Christians.

In settling a dispute over what kinds of foods were lawful for Christians to eat, the apostle Paul revealed that a person's conscience was under no authority but God Himself: "Why should my freedom be judged by another's conscience? If I take part in the meal with thankfulness, why am I denounced because of something I thank God for?" (1 Corinthians 10:29-30).

Your Walk   Jesus died for people from radically different cultural backgrounds. But unfortunately, believers sometimes judge each other based on cultural taboos rather than biblical principles.

God has set you, as well as all other believers, free from legalism. And so, honor Him by withholding judgments that go beyond the only legitimate judge of your actions: God's Word.

202

Freedom Versus Licentiousness

Read
GALATIANS 5:13-15

Freedom from sin is the opposite of freedom to sin.

Your World   "Really, now, professor, you can't be serious," chortled another panelist during a symposium on Christian ethics. The Christian professor had just presented a paper at the symposium in which he argued that homosexuality was expressly, consistently, and forcefully condemned in both the Old and New Testaments.

"Jesus set us free from the Draconian regulations of the Old Testament," continued the opposing panelist. "To resurrect them in the twentieth century is to take a giant step backward."

God's Word   People have been trying to pour Christian freedom into the mold of licentiousness for a long time. In fact, the apostle Paul warned the believers of Galatia not to fall prey to that temptation:

> You, my brothers, were called to be free. But do not use your freedom to indulge the sinful nature; rather, serve one another in love. The entire law is summed up in a single command: "Love your neighbor as yourself" (Galatians 5:13-14).

Your Walk   Christ set us free. But we dishonor Christ when we use our freedom to rationalize our sin.

Use your Christian freedom today to love a neighbor as yourself. Think of a member of your church who has a need. Love him or her as yourself by meeting that need in the name of the Lord. Do that, and you'll be using your freedom, rather than abusing it.

The Freedom of Obedience

Read
PSALM 119:44-45

He who runs in the path of God's commands has his heart set free.

Your World He had it all. Astonishing beauty. High position. The respect of his peers. The honor of his superior. The ability to do great and good things. If anyone in history was truly free, truly happy, truly privileged, it was Lucifer.

But something happened. Lucifer noticed that he wasn't the highest in rank. His Creator had authority over him. And Lucifer began to envy God, regarding submission to His authority as slavery, rather than freedom.

The result? Lucifer declared independence from God. But rather than freeing him from God, Lucifer's rebellion enslaved him in chains that will bind him forever.

God's Word Obedience is freedom. And though we do not rely on God's law for salvation, the New Testament exhorts us to use the law as a rule to guide us in free obedience to God's authority: "Do not merely listen to the word, and so deceive yourselves. Do what it says. . . . The man who looks intently into the perfect law that gives freedom . . . he will be blessed in what he does" (James 1:22,25).

Your Walk As you read Scripture, don't be content with just reading God's Word. Instead, seek to take one biblical principle each day and apply it to your life. By looking intently into God's Word and by obeying it, you will call down God's rich blessing in your life.

Freedom's Price

Read
REVELATION 1:4-6

Christ willingly gave His life to buy our freedom from sin.

You've heard the old maxim: "Anything that isn't worth dying for isn't worth living for."

A lot of wars have been fought in the name of freedom. Why? Because freedom is a cause for which people will pay the highest price: their own lives.

Christian freedom was also bought at a price—the highest price imaginable: the life and death of the Son of God. According to the apostle John, it was Christ's blood that bought His people freedom from their spiritual bondage: "To him who loves us and has freed us from our sins by his blood, and has made us to be a kingdom and priests to serve his God and Father—to him be glory and power for ever and ever!" (Revelation 1:5-6).

How did Christ free you from your sins by His blood? He subjected Himself to the bonds of Jewish religious leaders and Roman soldiers so you could be free from sin's chains. He faced the Father's wrath, experiencing the enslaving pains of hell, so you could live in freedom in heaven forever.

You have been set free from the penalty and power of sin. And when Jesus Christ returns, you will be set free from the very presence of sin.

The price of Christian freedom was Christ Himself. As you think about that during worship this weekend, respond like the apostle John: "To him be glory and power for ever and ever!"

205

Creativity

The Creator of the universe has given each one of us a drop or two of His *creativity.* A little creativity added to some of the most mundane chores can transform them into that which is exciting and productive.

That same creativity will enhance your relationship with God. Faith, prayer, and worship come vibrantly alive when your imagination and creativity are used according to God's design.

Try practicing some creativity during your quiet times this week.

Creativity: a Gift from the Creator

Read
GENESIS 1:27,31

*Christians
should live
artistically,
aesthetically,
and creatively.*

—Edith Schaeffer

Your World   Edith Schaeffer wrote in her book *Hidden Art:*

> What is creativity? We start with an idea, or a number of ideas. And we have to make a choice. We cannot do everything that comes into our minds. We are limited by time and by areas of talent and ability. Our creativity is not on God's level at all. His creativity is unlimited and infinite. Nevertheless we have been created in His image, so we can be and are made to be creative.

God's Word   Because every human being bears the image of God, everyone has the ability to create something beautiful and to appreciate it. "So God created man in his own image, in the image of God he created him. . . . God saw all that he had made, and it was very good" (Genesis 1:27, 31).

Your Walk   Artists, musicians, and writers are not the only people blessed with creativity. If you are human, you have some innate creative abilities.

Granted, some people are more creative than others, but creativity can be discovered in some of the most unlikely places: gardening, housework, plumbing, disciplining children, or even balancing a checkbook.

Do you think of yourself as a creative person? You are—whether you realize it or not.

This week we will explore the world of creativity and the Creator, who delights not only in His creation, but also in the beauty each one creates.

Everyone Loves to Hear a Story

Read
MATTHEW 13:1-23

No matter how old we are, stories spark a childlike faith in each of us that pleases God.

Your World "Once upon a time . . ." At the sound of those words, a hush blankets the room, and all attention is focused on the storyteller.

Why do we love stories? Not only do we often relate to the characters or the plot, but stories spark the imagination, the well of our creativity. We see ourselves in the shoes of the hero/heroine, the victim, or even the villain. When we do that, we enter another dimension and experience the progression of events ourselves.

And that is how we learn.

God's Word Madeleine L'Engle once said that Jesus Christ was not a theologian but a God who told stories.

"Then he told them many things in parables, saying: 'A farmer went out to sow his seed' " (Matthew 13:3).

Your Walk Stories reach both the hearts and minds of listeners. That is why Jesus Christ often taught in parables. He also used metaphors and symbols—many prophetic, all of them profound.

We have God's Word in black and white to tell us about God. But it is our imagination that helps us to see God majestically enthroned in heaven, angels rejoicing over each repentant sinner, or Jesus Christ nailed to a cross or rolling back the stone.

God knows that for you to have faith you must use your imagination. Try to serve and worship God without your imagination—it can't be done.

Inspire Creativity in Your Children

Read
PSALM 8

God has blessed your children with creativity. Help them discover it.

Your World In the early days of television, a favorite radio-turned-television show was Art Linkletter's *Kids Say the Darndest Things.* Mr. Linkletter knew that kids are innately creative, and millions of people tuned in every week to celebrate creativity born out of innocence.

God's Word As we see in the book *Children's Letters to God,* children have a delightfully unbridled approach to praising God.

From the lips of children and infants
you have ordained praise (Psalm 8:2).

Your Walk Creativity should be encouraged in children. Their creative spirits will thrive with your love and praise. And here are some other ideas:

- Show confidence in their abilities. Don't try to do everything for them.
- Allow them to take risks. It's called "creative freedom."
- Encourage make-believe play.
- Keep a selection of creative materials on hand: clay, paint, glue, yarn, etc.
- Value their creations. Display them in prominent places.
- Expose them to good books and limit television viewing.
- Avoid saying, "It won't work." Let them learn that on their own.
- Be a creative observer with your children. Take time to watch birds, raindrops, people, flowers, and animals.
- Encourage them to ask questions. A questioning mind is a creative mind.

Is All Art Worthy of Praise?

Read
EXODUS 31:1-11
PSALM 29:2

*In art,
we make visible
what God
has pictured
in our
imaginations.*
—Luci Shaw

Your World Is there really such a thing as bad art? Do any standards exist by which an artist's creation can be judged?

There is a raging controversy in our country over art. In recent years, Americans have seen an increasing trend that is not only considered obscene by most people, but blatantly blasphemous—all of it created by people created in the image of God.

Certainly the First Amendment protects any artist's right of freedom of expression; but should the work of these artists receive the same acclaim as, for instance, a Rembrandt painting or a Beethoven symphony?

God's Word Although God created us in His image, our creativity is tainted by sin. God commands us to strive for holiness in every aspect of our lives—including our creativity.

Worship the LORD in the beauty of holiness (Psalm 29:2 KJV).

Your Walk Do you recall that when our holy God finished His creation He called it "very good"? Can we deduce that sinners can create things that are very bad?

The next time you see or hear a work of art, ask yourself these questions:

- Does it glorify or degrade God?
- Does it celebrate God's creation or desecrate it?
- Does your spirit feel refreshed or grieved by it?
- Is it beautiful and holy?

211

Is Our Creativity Dis-appearing?

Read
COLOSSIANS 1:15-20

Creativity makes the ordinary extraordinary.

Your World Imagine life as a box of recipes with lists of ingredients and detailed instructions. There would be a recipe for marriage, business, politics, education, discipline, religion, relationships—every aspect of life.

We would never have to deal with the abstract, mysterious, or subjective. Emotions, perceptions, memories, and intuition would be unnecessary.

That's where our culture seems to be heading. We have exchanged creativity and imagination for television, video games, and entertainment gadgetry. Conversation, whimsy, and make-believe are vanishing from the lives of kids and adults. We are abandoning our creativity, settling for mediocrity, and spending thousands of dollars to avoid boredom.

God's Word Jesus Christ is our Standard-bearer and is the most creative Person who has ever lived.

> For by him all things were created: things in heaven and on earth, visible and invisible, whether thrones or powers or rulers or authorities; all things were created by him and for him. He is before all things, and in him all things hold together (Colossians 1:16-17).

Your Walk Do you think Jesus Christ ever gets bored? Impossible. He is the Author of creation and creativity.

Tomorrow we will look at ways you can tap into your God-given creativity. Until then, resolve to reject the mediocrity of a life void of creativity.

Your Creativity

Read
JOHN 16:17-33

Our creativity is bound only by our complacency.

In his book *A Whack on the Side of the Head,* Roger von Oech says: "We're more likely to respond [to a whack, i.e., losing a job] creatively if we've been chipping away at the 'mental locks' that close our minds."

Von Oech gives eight statements we blindly accept as truth. Creative people reject these assertions and "go for it":

1. *"Find the right answer."* We are taught from birth that only one answer exists. Explore the options.

2. *"That's not logical."* Instead of hard logic, create a metaphor to describe your problem and watch the solution surface.

3. *"Follow the rules."* Ignoring standards increases the possibility of new ideas.

4. *"Be practical."* Ask, "What if : . . ?"

5. *"Don't be foolish."* Humor can reveal the ambiguity of a situation. Play inspires creativity.

6. *"Don't make mistakes."* The founder of IBM said, "The way to succeed is to double your failure rate."

7. *"That's not my area."* Fresh ideas usually come from outside an area of specialization.

8. *"I'm not creative."* People who think they are creative are more so than those who don't think they are.

Are you like Moses? He doubted his ability to do God's will: "Who am I . . . ?" (Exodus 3:11).

Imagine if Moses, or Abraham, or the apostle Paul had believed these statements. Imagine what will happen to your creativity if you don't!

*God's
unconditional
love is
our secure
resting
place.*

Security in Christ

As God's children we thrive in His
unconditional love. He loves us so much that
He sent His Son, Jesus, to make it possible
for us to become His children. There is
no greater *security* than knowing that He
is our Father.

If you sometimes doubt the security of
your salvation, use your quiet times this
week to bask in the love of your
heavenly Father.

We Have Assurance Through Christ

Read
1 JOHN 4:18; 5:1-15

*I give them
eternal life,
and they shall
never perish;
no one can
snatch them out
of my hand.*

—Jesus

Your World Rose grew up in a strict, religious home in the 1930s and 1940s. She was told she must attend church several times a week, read her Bible and pray twice a day, and not consume certain foods or beverages on certain days or she would go to hell. Once, an adult in her church told her that God would punish her if she didn't brush her teeth correctly.

Today Rose's faith continues to be ruled by fear. In her community she is revered as a godly woman, yet she has no peace or joy because she has no assurance. *Sure, I might be saved today,* she thinks, *but what if I do something terrible tomorrow?* And at the age of 62, every time she brushes her teeth, she thinks about a capricious God who can't wait to unleash His wrath upon her.

God's Word Some people think that Christianity is like walking a tightrope without a net. One slip and it's over.

But the good news is that through Christ, we can have the assurance of eternal security: "I write these things to you who believe in the name of the Son of God so that you may know that you have eternal life" (1 John 5:13).

Your Walk Assurance breeds peace, which gives birth to joy, which generates love. But fear slays them all. This week we will look at some of the fears and misconceptions that surround God and the cross of Christ. Hope may be found in works, but assurance is found only in Christ.

216

Your Past, Present, and Future Sins

Read
2 CHRONICLES 30:9

*If one sin
or 100,000 sins
can cancel
your salvation,
then Jesus Christ
died in vain.*

Your World   At age 12, Kyle prayed to receive Jesus Christ as his Savior. Two weeks later he was baptized. For years Kyle's young faith grew. And at age 15 he stood before his church and announced his call to missions.

But Kyle never made it to the mission field. Instead, at age 31, he landed at the Oak Park Chemical Dependency Unit. There he met a pastor from a local church and eventually rededicated his life to the Lord.

Now, at age 34, Kyle is a man tormented by his past. His life is marked with the scars of the devastating sins that followed in the wake of his drug abuse. He believes God has forgiven the sins of the young Kyle, but doubts whether God will forgive a would-be missionary who neglected His call.

God's Word   Guilt is a healthy, natural consequence to sin. God uses it to discourage us from sinning. But Satan can also use it to devastate our faith. "This then is how we know that we belong to the truth, and how we set our hearts at rest in his presence whenever our hearts condemn us. For God is greater than our hearts, and he knows everything" (1 John 3:19-20).

Your Walk   The timing of our sins is irrelevant because, from the perspective of the cross, all of our sins were future sins. No sin in your past or future will surprise God. He saw all of them while hanging on the cross.

Adopted into the Family of God

Read
GALATIANS 4:4-5
EPHESIANS 1:3-5

There may be unwanted pregnancies, but there are never unwanted adoptions.

Your World Seven-year-old Timothy Cook is confused. At different times during his life, Timothy's parents have gently tried to explain, to one degree or another, the fact that he was adopted. No doubt about it, they told him, he is a Cook and will always be a Cook. The difference is that Timothy was not physically born into the family.

God's Word Hopefully, one day Timothy will understand the privilege of adoption, that his parents were motivated by love. He was wanted, and they willingly sacrificed for a child who was not of their flesh.

> The same is true in the family of God. For you did not receive a spirit that makes you a slave again to fear, but you received the Spirit of sonship. And by him we cry, "Abba, Father." The Spirit himself testifies with our spirit that we are God's children (Romans 8:15-16).

Your Walk Your heavenly Father loved you and wanted you to be His child from the beginning of time. And He sacrificed His only begotten Son for you to ensure that you would forever be His child.

As God's child, you won't be judged for your sins. That is one of the privileges of belonging to God's family. But the price was heavy: the cross. Rest secure that the cross is the official and irrevocable seal on your decree of heavenly adoption.

218

Joy and Love Are Free to Abound

Read
PSALM 91; JOHN 10:10

The light of Christ in your life may illumine the way for someone else.

Your World Joy and love radiate from Brenda like sunbeams. She's not even aware of it, but it's the first thing people notice when they see her. Therefore, people are often surprised when they discover that Brenda's life has been plagued with personal and physical pain.

Her secret? Every day Brenda makes the conscious decision to place her trust in Jesus Christ—nothing and no one else. He is her security.

God's Word Brenda is the first to admit that resting completely in Christ is not easy. It has taken her years of disciplined commitment to prayer and Scripture memorization.

Psalm 91 is one of the first Bible passages Brenda learned "by heart," and there it remains. "He who dwells in the shelter of the Most High will rest in the shadow of the Almighty. I will say of the LORD, 'He is my refuge and my fortress, my God, in whom I trust' " (Psalm 91:1-2).

Your Walk When you seek security in anything but Christ, then fear, worry, bitterness, guilt, jealousy, or self-pity seem to control your life. It's a part of walking in darkness.

Only when you release the cares of your life into the hands of Christ is the Holy Spirit free to express His joy and love, along with all His other fruit, through you to the world around you. It's a part of walking in the light.

What About the Unpardonable Sin?

Read
MATTHEW 12:31-32
ROMANS 10

There is no unpardonable sin, but there is an unpardonable state: unbelief.

Your World Ross's heart is pounding and his stomach is in knots. He has just read Matthew 12:31-32 and is afraid he has committed the unpardonable sin: "blasphemy against the Spirit."

Why? In college his fraternity performed a skit mocking a television faith healer. Ross wrote the skit and played the role of the faith healer. The crowd howled as Ross gyrated around his "patient" and rebuked the demons with a shrill "in the nay-em of Jeee-zuh-hus!" Now, three years later and a new believer, Ross fears a past indiscretion has destroyed any hope for his salvation.

God's Word Blasphemy against the Holy Spirit is the only unforgivable sin found in the Bible. However, many biblical scholars maintain that it is impossible to commit the sin today because Christ is not present in the flesh. The Pharisees were guilty of the dreaded sin because they witnessed the evidence that Jesus was the Messiah, but they still accused Him of having a satanic spirit.

Besides, God does not exclude anyone or any sin from His grace. "Everyone who calls on the name of the Lord will be saved" (Romans 10:13).

Your Walk No matter how wicked your past, God will forgive you. He forgave David's adultery, dishonesty, and murder, the prodigal's "partying," Peter's denial and profanity, and Paul's persecution of believers. He will certainly forgive you.

Blessed Assurance

Read
JOHN 14:27
HEBREWS 10:22

We can be assured of God's unconditional love that gave us the gift of salvation.

We are secure in Christ. Charles Stanley writes in his book *Eternal Security: Can You Be Sure?:*

> I have never met a Christian who had lost his salvation. However, I have met plenty who had lost their assurance. Our security rests in the hands of an unconditionally loving, heavenly Father. One who gave His best to ensure our fellowship with Him forever. Our assurance rests in understanding and accepting these glorious truths.

Some Christians lack the assurance they desperately need. Sometimes this may be due to erroneous teaching or stifled guilt. But when a believer has no assurance, his or her relationship with God is marred by instability.

God, in His perfect wisdom, designed us to fit in permanent and precise balance with the cross. When we acknowledge that our security is in the cross of Christ, our lives are set on a firm foundation of faith and stability. Then the Holy Spirit is free to bear His fruit in our lives. "The fruit of righteousness will be peace; the effect of righteousness will be quietness and confidence forever" (Isaiah 32:17).

Fanny Crosby, author of an estimated 8000 gospel songs, sums it up beautifully in this hymn:

> Blessed assurance, Jesus is mine!
> Oh what a foretaste of glory divine.
> Heir of salvation, purchase of God.
> Born of His Spirit, washed in His blood.

Are you secure in that truth?

*If you
enjoy verbal
battle,
it's time
to hold
your tongue.*

Criticism

We've all experienced it: the kind of
criticism that's downright nasty. It's mean.
It's cruel. It's designed to destroy us emotionally.
It cuts. It hurts. It wounds. It makes us feel like
we've hit rock bottom.

That's the kind of criticism that comes
naturally to all of us. We feel insecure about
ourselves, and so we like to lash out and bring
other people down.

But there's another kind of criticism—
constructive criticism—that is meant to build
people up. In your quiet times this week,
find out how to avoid the former and
practice the latter.

No Complaining or Arguing

Read
PHILIPPIANS 2:12-16

Constant grumbling is like a constant dripping: After a while, it can drive you crazy.

Your World Have you ever known someone with a critical spirit? Someone who was never satisfied, regardless of how you tried to please him or her?

There's almost nothing worse than a boss, a fellow employee, a spouse, a child, a parent, or a friend who can't seem to say anything unless it's negative, rude, or down-right cruel.

God's Word Here's the problem with destructive criticism: It never builds anybody up; it always degrades and destroys both its giver and receiver.

And so, the apostle Paul was clear and blunt. Believers should always avoid a destructive, critical spirit:

> Do everything without complaining or arguing, so that you may become blameless and pure, children of God without fault in a crooked and depraved generation, in which you shine like stars in the universe as you hold out the word of life (Philippians 2:14-16).

Your Walk Paul emphasizes that not complaining and not arguing is part of being an example of purity to an impure world. A critical spirit, then, undermines a person's witness to a world hungry for kindness. For if the Christian faith is powerless to calm a person's criticism, how much power does it have for real life-change? The answer is obvious: None.

If you struggle with a critical spirit, use your quiet times this week to ask God to help you change, for the sake of your witness in His world.

The Biggest Critic of All

Read
JOB 1:1-11

*Satan is,
always has been,
and always will be
a critic and
a liar.*

Your World Picture the scenario. You do good work, and everybody knows it. You regard your job as God's calling, not merely as a paycheck. And the company has benefited often from your willingness to go the second mile.

But someone has been watching you—someone who doesn't like the rewards you've gotten for your labor. And this someone goes to the company president and criticizes you unfairly in an attempt to undermine his confidence in you.

God's Word In a sense, that's what happens to you every day. Satan, whose name means "accuser," is constantly criticizing you before God. We have a record of Satan's criticism in the first chapter of the Book of Job:

> "Does Job fear God for nothing?" Satan [said]. "Have you not put a hedge around him and his household and everything he has? You have blessed the work of his hands, so that his flocks and herds are spread throughout the land. But stretch out your hand and strike everything he has, and he will surely curse you to your face" (Job 1:9-11).

Your Walk Satan is criticizing you right now. But you don't have to worry. Jesus, whose testimony carries far more weight with the Father, is defending you even as you read.

Follow Jesus' example. Defend those for whom He died. Leave the criticizing to the devil. A time is coming when he will criticize no more.

Criticism and God's Wrath

Read
EXODUS 17:1-7

Criticism isn't just harmful to others; God hates it.

Your World   "Mommy, you never give me anything," four-year-old James complains with arms folded tightly and face pouting. Surrounding James and his mother is a room filled with toys, books, a desk and easel, and a dozen stuffed animals.

"Mommy, you never love me," James says, five minutes after his mother has hugged him for the third time that morning.

God's Word   We expect children to complain. But when adults complain censoriously, we don't regard it as cute.

The Israelites criticized Moses viciously—even after witnessing some of the most astonishing miracles recorded in Scripture. And the apostle Paul warned the Corinthian church that such criticism deserves severe punishment: "God was not pleased with most of [our forefathers]; their bodies were scattered over the desert. . . . And do not grumble, as some of them did—and were killed by the destroying angel" (1 Corinthians 10:5,10).

Your Walk   God was not pleased with the Israelites because they would not trust Him. They disobeyed His commands, and they complained about His leading in their lives.

Learn from their mistakes. Obey God with joy, and be content with His providence in your life. He has a good reason for you being exactly where you are. Complaining about it grieves Him greatly.

Criticism in the Home

Read
1 PETER 3:1-12

Nobody likes an overly critical mom or dad.

Your World As a child, you probably said, "Sticks and stones may break my bones, but names will never hurt me." You didn't tell the truth. Unjust and harmful criticism hurts as bad or worse than physical wounds. A broken bone heals in weeks. A broken heart sometimes lasts a lifetime.

Criticism has the power to hurt deeply—especially in the home, where people are completely intimate and thus completely vulnerable.

God's Word The apostle Peter gives guidelines about how family members should treat each other. He calls us to be compassionate, not critical:

> All of you, live in harmony with one another; be sympathetic, love as brothers, be compassionate and humble. Do not repay evil with evil or insult with insult, but with blessing, because to this you were called so that you may inherit a blessing. For, "Whoever would love life and see good days must keep his tongue from evil and his lips from deceitful speech" (1 Peter 3:8-10).

Your Walk When your family describes you to others, do they say you are sympathetic and compassionate . . . or cynical and critical? If you struggle with being overly critical of your family, look for things to praise. Regardless of how small the area is, find something to praise about each of your family members every day. Soon that one small praise will grow to many compliments.

Constructive Criticism

Read
EPHESIANS 4:15-16

Go ahead and criticize— but only constructively.

Your World So far this week, we've talked only about destructive criticism. But that isn't the only kind of criticism there is. Constructive criticism is to our spiritual selves what pain is to our bodies: It alerts us that something isn't right. It warns us that we have a problem that needs to be fixed.

God's Word Destructive criticism tears down. Constructive criticism builds up. The Bible forbids the former and encourages the latter.

In fact, according to the apostle Paul, constructive criticism among the body of Christ is essential to our spiritual growth:

> Speaking the truth in love, we will in all things grow up into him who is the Head, that is, Christ. From him the whole body, joined and held together by every supporting ligament, grows and builds itself up in love, as each part does its work (Ephesians 4:15-16).

Your Walk Speak the truth in love, Paul says. If you are a person who has trouble speaking truth if it's painful to the hearer, take heed to Paul's words. Go ahead and encourage a fellow believer to train his or her children more faithfully, to read the Bible more regularly, to seek more sanctified entertainment habits.

If you are a person who has trouble speaking in love, take heed to Paul's words. Remember that the truth should build up, not tear down, and temper your comments accordingly.

Jesus' Method

Read
JOHN 4:1-26

Speaking the truth in love is the most effective form of criticism.

Jesus knew how to use criticism to build people up rather than to tear them down. He never pulled punches with truth; He always did what was best for those to whom He spoke.

When Jesus sat at Jacob's well, He knew the spiritual condition of the woman drawing water. He knew why she waited until much later than other village women to draw her daily water. He knew she was ashamed, and He knew why.

But Jesus didn't blast the woman with the fact that she was a sinner living with a man out of wedlock, though that would have been the truth. Nor did He keep silent about the woman's sin so as not to hurt her feelings. That would have been an act of kindness, but not love.

Instead, He waited for precisely the right moment, and then He gently and lovingly let her know that He knew the truth:

> He told her, "Go, call your husband and come back." "I have no husband," she replied. Jesus said to her, "You are right when you say you have no husband. The fact is, you have had five husbands, and the man you now have is not your husband. What you have just said is quite true" (John 4:16-18).

That's speaking the truth in love. That's constructive criticism. And the result? The woman believed in Jesus. And because of her testimony, many other people believed.

Go and do likewise. Speak the truth. But do so to build up others around you.

*No one
can make you
feel inferior
without your
consent.*

Self-Esteem

In a society where everyone is so "self-aware," why is *self-esteem* still such an issue? The truth is that we are constantly confronted with images that tear down the person we attempt to build up.

But when God constructs our identity, when He is the central foundation on which our "self" is built, then we truly become the unique person He made us to be. We display His character, not the character of the latest supermodel or Hollywood star.

The source of your identity is your relationship with Christ. Let that fact boost your self-image this week.

Desiring Intimacy and Impact

Read
GENESIS 1:27-28

At the Fall, self-esteem was lost. In heaven, self-esteem will be perfect once again.

Your World   Mark Twain said, "When people do not respect us we are offended; yet deep down in his private heart no man much respects himself."

C. S. Lewis said, "Unless Christianity is wholly false, the perception of ourselves which we have in moments of shame must be the only true one."

God's Word   From the beginning of human history, people were created by God to have an intimate relationship with Him and a significant impact on His world: "Then God said, 'Let us make man in our image, in our likeness, and let them rule over . . . all the earth' " (Genesis 1:26).

Our first parents didn't worry about self-esteem. Their intimacy with God and their impact on His world were vital, complete, and significant.

But when Adam and Eve sinned, God broke intimacy with them and cursed their work. From then on, they could only long for the sense of security and significance they once possessed.

Your Walk   Do you long for a relationship of deep intimacy? Do you long to have an impact on the world around you? You're not alone. All of Adam's children have thirsts that only the Lord can quench.

Christ died to right the wrongs of the Fall. Through Him, you can travel the road back to the self-esteem that comes from intimacy with God and having an impact on His world.

What God Thinks About You

Read
EPHESIANS 3:14-19

Believe what God says about you, and what you think about yourself will change.

Your World A gunslinger in the wild West burst into a saloon with both guns blazing. He yelled, "All you dirty skunks get outta here!"

The saloon cleared immediately. But when the smoke cleared, one lone man stood at the bar, calmly sipping his drink. The gunslinger looked him in the eye and demanded, "Well?"

"Well," answered the man, "there sure was a lot of them, warn't there?"

God's Word We all have probably thought of ourselves as dirty skunks—and maybe even worse.

But this is the miracle of our faith: God, though He knows us even better than we know ourselves, still loves us and wants our fellowship and friendship.

> Put your hope in the LORD, for with the LORD is unfailing love and with him is full redemption (Psalm 130:7).

Your Walk Real self-esteem cannot be based on an illusion. No matter how hard you try to convince yourself of how wonderful you are, you know that apart from God's grace it isn't true.

But self-esteem can come from contemplating how deeply God loves you. Close your eyes and imagine Christ on the cross. God's turning away from His Son was proof of His great love for you.

God became a man and suffered on the cross so that you could be with Him forever. Let that assurance sink deep into your heart, and you won't consider yourself a dirty skunk anymore.

Trust the Maker's Product

Read
PSALM 139:1-16

Acknowledge that God made you, and you will one day accept the way He made you.

Your World   Jimmy Durante built a comic reputation on the size of his nose. But even though that nose made him so much money, it bothered him all his life.

He once said,

> Every time I went down the street I'd hear, "Look at da big-nosed kid." And if they said nothin', nothin' at all, I'd shrivel up and think they was sayin', "What an ugly kid!" Even when I am makin' a fortune on account of the big beak, and while I am out there on stage, laughin' and kiddin' about the nose, at no time was I ever happy about it.

God's Word   But the Lord assures us that it is He who has made us. The physical, mental, and emotional aspects of our personalities are the deliberate and conscious work of God: "For you created my inmost being; you knit me together in my mother's womb" (Psalm 139:13).

What a mystery! God formed each of us in the womb—carefully, lovingly, and deliberately knitting us together, body and soul.

Your Walk   Your body and personality are the creation of One who is all-wise, all-loving, completely good, and all-powerful— in a word, perfect. While you aren't perfect because of the effects of sin, you are still the result of the thought and work of Him who never makes mistakes. Comfort yourself in this: You can trust the One who made you.

An Attitude of Humble Service

Read
PHILIPPIANS 2:1-11

Loving others is sometimes the key to learning to love yourself correctly.

Your World In his book *The Winning Attitude,* John C. Maxwell points out that airplanes have an instrument called the "attitude indicator." The attitude indicator lets the pilot know how the plane is flying in relation to the horizon.

When the airplane is climbing, it has a nose-high attitude—the nose of the aircraft is pointed above the horizon. Conversely, when the aircraft is diving, it has a nose-down attitude. Change the plane's attitude, and you change the way it flies.

God's Word Change a person's attitude, and you change the way he or she lives. The apostle Paul encourages us to change our attitudes according to the standard set by the ultimate attitude indicator: Jesus Christ:

> Do nothing out of selfish ambition or vain conceit, but in humility consider others better than yourselves. Each of you should look not only to your own interests, but also to the interests of others. Your attitude should be the same as that of Christ Jesus (Philippians 2:3-5).

Your Walk Jesus' life was spent with an attitude of humble service to God and people. And He certainly wasn't a man of low self-esteem.

If you have trouble realizing your self-worth, try volunteering at a convalescent home, inner-city mission, AIDS hospice, or preschool. Looking to the interests of other people is a good way to look to your own interests.

Bless and You Shall Be Blessed

Read
1 PETER 4:7-11

True service isn't how many people you help but how well you help where God has you.

Your World   Dr. Arthur E. Morgan said, "Lack of something to feel important about is almost the greatest tragedy a man may have." An anonymous proverbialist added to the idea when he or she said, "The forests would be silent indeed, if no birds sang except those who sang best."

God's Word   For all Christians, from the least to the greatest, an important ingredient of healthy self-esteem is service—as these words of the apostle Peter remind us:

> Each one should use whatever gift he has received to serve others, faithfully administering God's grace in its various forms (1 Peter 4:10).

By using our spiritual gifts to serve God's kingdom, we gain a powerful sense of accomplishment. Participating in the Spirit's work brings a profound sense of self-satisfaction.

Your Walk   Are you using the abilities God has given you? Whether it's speaking before a crowd of 1000, helping a child learn to read, or preparing the elements for the worship communion, our gifts are important. They're one way God has chosen to enable you to contribute to and feel a part of the big picture of His work.

When you use your gifts, you not only bless others, but you are blessed; you not only encourage others, but you are encouraged; you not only make others feel that they matter, you feel that you matter—and you do.

Heaven's Way

Read
JOHN 14:6

*Let God
undo the
damage Satan
has done
in your heart.*

Shelomon, a Hasidic rabbi, asked, "What is the worst thing an evil urge can achieve?" He answered, "To make man forget that he is the son of a King."

Satan would tell Christians that they are fools and cripples—useless and gross eyesores on the landscape of the living. He would keep every Christian from ever exercising his rights as a child of God. How then do we rid ourselves of the debilitating, angry darts that Satan fires into our minds?

Listen to the cry of King David: "Search me, O God, and know my heart; test me and know my anxious thoughts. See if there is any offensive way in me, and lead me in the way everlasting" (Psalm 139:23-24). It's an invitation to God to work in our hearts, to expose and then scour away the mildew of false, heartbreaking thoughts.

David wants us to do more than tell ourselves we're worthwhile (as if simply telling ourselves something would actually make us believe it). Rather, David encourages us to ask God to transform us from the inside out so that all worthless, denigrating, cheap, and hateful thoughts are banished.

Only through this kind of radical transformation can we become the beautiful creations of God, both inside and outside, that He meant for us to be. Praise God that He transforms us from self-haters into healthy self-esteemers as He leads us in the Way everlasting: His Son.

*A man
without
purpose
is like a
ship without
a rudder.*

Purpose

"Why?" It's a young child's favorite word. But as children of God, we ask "why" so often so we can discover a reason or *purpose* for our actions. It's a characteristic of leading an examined life before Christ. Sometimes we need to take a moment and regain our focus, our sense of purpose, to ask why we do what we do. For our own gain or to serve Christ?

This week, use your quiet times to thank God for His purpose in your life.

God's Purpose: Cosmic Redemption

Read
COLOSSIANS 1:19-20

God's purpose? To make all things right, both in heaven and on earth.

Your World Abraham Kuyper, Dutch theologian and statesman of the late 1800s, said, "There is not a thumb-breadth of the universe about which Christ does not say, 'It is mine.'" Since the King of kings is sovereign over every molecule of the universe, history is truly His story. The morning *Times* is filled with eternities—eternal purposes accomplished in time.

God's Word According to the apostle Paul, God's purpose in history is nothing less than total victory, universal renewal, cosmic redemption:

> He made known to us the mystery of his will according to his good pleasure, which he purposed in Christ, to be put into effect when the times will have reached their fulfillment—to bring all things in heaven and on earth together under one head, even Christ (Ephesians 1:9-10).

Your Walk In countless ways, God is using the free choices of His creatures to move His story to completion. Everything you do, even something as mundane as eating breakfast, fits into God's purpose (1 Corinthians 10:31).

The question then isn't whether you will fit into God's purpose. The question is, How will you fit in? Will you be a servant or a rebel?

Being a servant demands commitment to growing in God's Word, giving Him your worship, and doing good works. In doing those things, you serve Christ, adding your chapter to His story.

No God? No Purpose!

Read
1 CORINTHIANS 15:32

Humankind's purpose? Strictly "under the sun," there is none.

Your World In his book *Three Philosophies of Life,* Peter Kreeft writes:

The modern West . . . is the first [civilization] that does not have or teach its citizens any answer to the question why they exist. . . . A more candid way of saying the same thing is that our society has nothing but its own ignorance to give us on this, the most important of all questions. As society grows, it . . . knows more about the little things and less about the big things. It knows more about every thing and less about Everything.

God's Word The plight of modern humankind isn't so modern. Thousands of years ago, the writer of Ecclesiastes taught that life lived strictly "under the sun" (in other words, without God) is purposeless:

"Meaningless! Meaningless!" says the Teacher. "Utterly meaningless! Everything is meaningless." . . . I have seen all the things that are done under the sun; all of them are meaningless, a chasing after the wind (Ecclesiastes 1:2, 14).

Your Walk How sad. All of your relatives, friends, and business associates who believe only in what they can see, hear, and feel are living lives that are ultimately purposeless.

But you as a Christian know your life has an end (purpose), not just an end (finish). That should cause your heart to rejoice so much that other people will feel compelled to ask you why you seem to have such hope.

Heaven— the Highest Good

Read
JOHN 14:1-4

Keeping your heavenly goal in mind keeps your earthly walk in line.

Your World Have you heard it said that so-and-so is so heavenly minded that he's no earthly good? That's impossible. In fact, the more heavenly minded a person is, the more earthly good he will be.

To see God, to serve Him in the new heaven and new earth for eternity, is the *summum bonum,* the highest good, the ultimate purpose of human existence.

God's Word Just as those who purpose to get to work on time set their clocks, those who purpose to live with God in heaven set their walks accordingly.

When people become believers, their change in purpose causes a radical change in their lives: "You turned to God from idols to serve the living and true God, and to wait for his Son from heaven" (1 Thessalonians 1:9-10).

Your Walk Having heaven as your purpose gives you more, not less, to do in this world. Jesus didn't pray, "May Your will be ignored on earth since the goal is heaven"; He said, "Your will be done on earth as it is in heaven" (Matthew 6:10).

When colonists settled the New World, those who loved their mother country most worked hardest to make their colony like home. Consider yourself a colonist from heaven; work to make your world more like your heavenly home.

The Purpose of the Church: Frangelism

Read
MATTHEW 28:18-20

Frangelism is friends witnessing to friends— for their best Friend's sake.

Your World According to Bill and Amy Stearns in their book *Catch the Vision 2000,* God is doing amazing things in world evangelism:

- In A.D. 100, there were 360 non-Christians in the world for every believer. Today the ratio is about 7 to 1.

- Since 1980, more Muslims in Iran have come to Christ than in the last 1000 years combined.

- In 1950, there were about one million believers in China. Today there are more than 60 million.

- Africa, just three percent Christian in 1900, is over 40 percent Christian today.

God's Word Just before Jesus ascended into heaven, He clearly revealed His purpose for the church: We are to be His witnesses throughout the earth. "You will receive power when the Holy Spirit comes on you; and you will be my witnesses in Jerusalem, and in all Judea and Samaria, and to the ends of the earth" (Acts 1:8).

Your Walk Try practicing friendship evangelism—also known as frangelism. Frangelism is relational, not confrontational, outreach—and it works.

According to one study, 85 percent of Christians who were led to Christ by a friend were still active in their faith six months later. But 85 percent of those who professed Christ after being confronted by a stranger had fallen away.

Be a frangelist. Invite a non-Christian to church this weekend.

Conformed to the Likeness of Christ

Read
ROMANS 8:28-30

God predestined the cross, but Jesus still had to walk from Jerusalem to Calvary.

Your World   Question: Left completely to yourself, how long do you think you would last in your efforts to fulfill God's purpose for your life?

Answer: Not long at all.

God's Word   According to the apostle Paul, God's purpose for His people is that they become more like their Master. And God will make sure His purpose is fulfilled.

> For those God foreknew he also predestined to be conformed to the likeness of his Son, that he might be the firstborn among many brothers (Romans 8:29).

Your Walk   Does that mean you can sit passively, waiting for God to do something completely apart from your will? Of course not. You have a vital part to play in God's fulfilling of His purpose.

God has graciously made available all you need to help you make Christlike decisions. And it's up to you, by the power of the Holy Spirit, to take advantage of the many ways God has provided to help you in your Christian walk.

Do you want to be more like God's one and only Son? Start by reading the Bible regularly, praying for God's assistance constantly, worshiping Him fervently, and fellowshipping with His people honestly.

Just as a potter uses tools to conform a piece of clay to a preconceived shape, God uses these tools to conform you to the likeness of His Son. And that is cause to rejoice.

Hope
for the
Lonely

Read
PSALM 46

*A man
without purpose
is like a
ship without
a rudder.*

Let's face it: Suffering—invasive, destructive, tormenting, painful—comes to everyone.

Generation after generation, we try to understand our pain. After all, if God loves us as much as He says, why do we suffer?

Even a righteous man like Job suffered horribly. He lost everything: wealth, family, health. Why?

Job's friends had an answer: "Bad things don't really happen to good people. Therefore, people who suffer trials are really bad. Since Job is suffering, he needs to repent," they reasoned. Presto. Problem solved.

Job knew his friends were wrong. He knew that, as far as he was able, he was a righteous man.

So why did he suffer if he was righteous? Job came up with his own answer: "God must be unjust." Presto. Problem solved.

Not quite.

God's only answer to Job in the midst of his suffering was that God, not Job, created and controls the universe. Job would have to accept the trials without understanding why for the time being.

Sometimes this is the only answer we can have in the midst of our own trials. We simply have to trust that God is so powerful and so good that He will ultimately accomplish His purpose to make all things in the universe right.

And we simply have to trust that God loves us so much He uses whatever means necessary—even His Son's suffering and our own—to make us right with Him. Thank God that He's in charge and His purposes will be accomplished.

*The Beatitudes
describe the
blessings
that belong to
those who
live in the
kingdom of God.*

Beatitudes

As the prologue of Christ's Sermon
on the Mount, the *Beatitudes* form the
Constitution, so to speak, for the kingdom of
heaven. In them Jesus describes the attitudes
of heart and life that please our eternal
King and Father when they are present
in the lives of His children.

This week why not ask the Holy Spirit
to use this study of the Beatitudes to help you
assess your spiritual condition. You'll be
blessed if you do!

The Blessedness of Union with God

Read
PSALM 84:4-5

*Happiness
that is strictly
a feeling
is always
elusive.*

Your World Happiness is every human being's relentless pursuit. But not everyone's idea of happiness is the same.

For most people in our era, happiness is strictly subjective—a warm feeling. But true happiness is much more. It is an objective state, not merely a subjective feeling. It is a condition of being in union with God, giving Him glory and receiving His favor.

God's Word The Bible says a lot about such a condition. But in describing it, Scripture doesn't usually use the word *happy*; it uses the word *blessed*.

The first section of the Sermon on the Mount, which we call "the Beatitudes," reveals that true happiness is found in walking with God. It is the same message as found throughout Scripture.

> Blessed is the man who does not walk in the counsel of the wicked or stand in the way of sinners or sit in the seat of mockers. But his delight is in the law of the LORD, and on his law he meditates day and night (Psalm 1:1-2).

Your Walk Every person, including you, wants to be happy. God made us to desire His presence, His favor, His glory. In other words, He made us to deeply desire true happiness.

As a believer, be content in this: Regardless of your circumstances, you have the promise of God that one day you will experience true happiness in its fullness. You will walk with God. Ponder that and give thanks.

Humble Saints Are God's Heroes

Read
JAMES 4:10

Humble saints are blessed with God's presence and power.

Your World From the human perspective, the work of the apostles is mystifying. These relatively unknown Hebrew men turned the world upside down.

From the human perspective, Mother Teresa was paradoxical. We are astonished that a small, frail, seemingly unexceptional woman could do so much for so many with so little.

The apostles and Mother Teresa have something in common: They are responsible for great acts done in humble service to God.

God's Word When God works, He enlists people to work with Him. And there is one basic requirement for joining God's team: humility.

According to Jesus, those who know that they desperately need God will be blessed with 1) God's presence, and 2) God's help in effectively doing His work.

> Blessed are the poor in spirit, for theirs is the kingdom of heaven. Blessed are those who mourn, for they will be comforted. Blessed are the meek, for they will inherit the earth (Matthew 5:3-5).

Your Walk Imagine feeling God's presence on a daily basis. Imagine doing great works for God.

You can make real what you've just imagined. Humble yourself before God. Give Him the praise He deserves. Acknowledge that apart from Him you can do nothing. And fervently ask Him to work His will through you.

The High Price of Mercy

Read
Luke 10:25-37

*Mercy costs
a lot, yet
delivers
much more.*

Your World   "You have been found guilty, Mr. Jones," the judge said as he peered over his glasses. "Because this is your first offense, I will give you the minimum sentence: You are hereby fined $2500."

"But I can't pay, Your Honor."

"Then you will spend two years in jail."

As Mr. Jones speechlessly pondered his fate, a man stood up in the courtroom and said, "I'll pay the fine, Your Honor." After consultation, the judge accepted the man's payment, and Mr. Jones went free.

God's Word   True mercy always comes with a price. God can be merciful to us, but at an incredibly high cost: His Son's death.

Jesus was rewarded for His merciful act of dying on a cross. He was raised from the dead and seated at the right hand of God. Similarly, those of us who are merciful to others will experience God's mercy both in this life and the next: "Blessed are the merciful, for they will be shown mercy" (Matthew 5:7).

Your Walk   In God's moral universe, it truly is more blessed to give than to receive. Only those who are turned inward don't see that.

If you know someone who is hurting in a way you can help, be merciful. It may cost you, but God can be trusted. When He says the merciful are blessed, blessed they truly are. And blessed you truly will be.

Peace with God; Peace with Man

Read
ISAIAH 9:6

Blessed are those in whose hearts the Prince of peace reigns.

Your World   In his book *Back to Virtue,* Peter Kreeft writes,

> Peace, says Augustine, is not merely the absence of war. Peace is positive. It is rest in our [purpose]. After the stone falls, it is at peace. After the acorn grows into the oak tree, it is at peace in its treehood and does not grow any further. After the animal's hunger is sated with food, it is at peace. And the human heart? Because "thou has made us for thyself," therefore "our hearts are restless until they rest in thee." For man, peace is another word for God.

God's Word   Because God is man's true purpose, peace with God is man's most important—and most satisfying—pursuit. And a person who is at peace with God is at peace with others.

> Blessed are the peacemakers, for they will be called sons of God (Matthew 5:9).

Notice that the passage doesn't say, "Blessed are the peacemakers, for they will earn the right to call God their Father." Peace with God doesn't result from being at peace with men; God's peace produces peace in His people.

Your Walk   Are you at peace with God? Are you at peace with other people?

Jesus says we should make peace before we offer our gifts at God's altar (Matthew 5:23). If someone has something against you, make peace with that person before you go to worship this weekend. Obey Jesus' words, and people will know you are a son (or daughter) of God.

Persecuted for Righteous- ness

Read
JOHN 15:19-20

*Truth-speakers
may be cursed
in this world,
but they'll be
blessed in
the next.*

Your World   In modern America, God's Word is out of favor. As a result, the word *sin* is out of fashion.

Homosexuality isn't a sin; it's an alternative life-style. Adultery isn't a sin; it just happens. Fornication isn't sin; it's the right thing to do for two people who want to get to know each other.

There are, however, still some "sins" left in the modern world. Religious fanaticism, for example. And to claim that every area of life—and therefore every person—is subject to the teaching of the Bible is certainly fanatical.

God's Word   Jesus called people to repentance. And He paid the ultimate price for such "fanatical" behavior. We shouldn't be surprised, then, when we, Jesus' followers, have to endure persecution for imitating our Master:

> Blessed are you when people insult you, persecute you and falsely say all kinds of evil against you because of me. Rejoice and be glad, because great is your reward in heaven, for in the same way they persecuted the prophets who were before you (Matthew 5:11-12).

Your Walk   Have you heard of the "winsomeness syndrome"? A lot of believers have it. They're so interested in presenting truth in an inoffensive way, their "truth" can become half-truth.

There's no getting around it: Truth can be offensive, even when spoken in love. Speak truth, and rejoice. If you're persecuted, you're in good company.

The Ultimate Blessing

Read
HEBREWS 12:14

*To be pure
in heart
you must have
a new heart
that only
Jesus Christ
can give.
Do you?*

As we've seen this week, living in communion with God through His Son, Jesus Christ, brings what all people seek: happiness. Not merely feel-good happiness. Real happiness. Objective happiness. The blessedness only God can give.

And there is coming a time when God's children will experience complete happiness. For we will experience God Himself in His fullness.

While we still live on this earth, while we still walk this pilgrimage, we can experience happiness only in a limited way. We have sinned, and we know God only by means of His revelation—the Word He has spoken and the world He has made.

But a time swiftly approaches when we will no longer wear the blinders of sin. Instead, "when he appears, we shall be like him, for we shall see him as he is" (1 John 3:2).

We shall see Him as He is. We shall see God face-to-face. Finally, the promise to Abraham and his descendants will be completed: "Now the dwelling of God is with men, and he will live with them. They will be his people, and God himself will be with them and be their God" (Revelation 21:3). And then, the ultimate Beatitude will be fully realized: "Blessed are the pure in heart, for they will see God" (Matthew 5:8).

Are you ready? It's going to be a blessed eternity. Let the blessings begin as you worship Him.

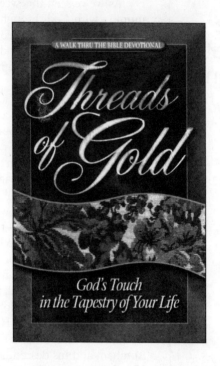

Walk Thru the Bible Ministries

Walk Thru the Bible Ministries (WTB) began in the early 1970s when a young teacher named Bruce Wilkinson developed an innovative way of teaching surveys of the Bible. From these small beginnings emerged a multifaceted Bible-teaching ministry. By focusing on the central themes of Scripture and their practical application, WTB has wide acceptance in denominations and fellowships around the world. In addition, it has carefully developed alliances with over 100 Christian organizations. WTB has four major ministries:

International Ministries

WTB's International Ministry extends to over 70 countries, representing some 50 languages. With recent advances, WTB now has more than 3,000 trained seminar instructors worldwide. International branch offices are located in Australia, Great Britain, Singapore, New Zealand, South Africa, and Ukraine.

WTB Publishing

The Publishing Ministry began in 1978 with the launching of *The Daily Walk* magazine. WTB publications enable individuals and families to maintain a meaningful habit of daily devotional time in the Word of God. The publications include *Closer Walk, Family Walk, YouthWalk, LifeWalk,* and *Tapestry.*

WTB Seminars and Leadership Training

People of all ages develop a deeper understanding of the Bible through WTB's unique Old and New Testament surveys. Other seminars offered include: *The Seven Laws of the Learner, Teaching with Style,* and *The Biblical Portrait of Marriage.* The Leadership Training Ministry goes into secular business as well as churches and Christian organizations to communicate biblical principles of leadership. Each training module provides practical tools that make biblical truth relevant both in personal relationships and in the marketplace.

LifeChange Videos

The WTB creative team has developed a number of dynamic video courses for training leaders and for personal growth including: *The Biblical Portrait of Marriage, The Seven Laws of the Learner,* and *Personal Holiness in Times of Temptation.* Video makes it possible to bring WTB's lifechanging Bible teaching into churches and homes throughout the world.

No matter what the ministry, no matter where the ministry, WTB focuses on the Word of God and encourages people of all nations to grow in their knowledge of God and unreserved obedience and serve to Him. For more information about Walk Thru the Bible's publications, videos, or seminars in your area, contact Walk Thru the Bible Ministries, 4201 North Peachtree Road, Atlanta, GA 30341-1207 or call (770) 458-9300. Visit our web site at www.walkthru.org